EVEREST

Reflections From The Top

Edited by
Christine Gee, Garry Weare
and Margaret Gee

RRIDER BOOKS

RIDER

LONDON · SYDNEY · AUCKLAND · JOHANNESBURG

1 3 5 7 9 10 8 6 4 2

This paperback edition published in 2013

First published in 2003 by Rider, an imprint of Ebury Publishing

Ebury Publishing is a Random House Group company

The Random House Group Limited Reg. No. 954009

Addresses for companies within the Random House Group can be found at:
www.randomhouse.co.uk

A CIP catalogue record for this book is
available from the British Library

The Random House Group Limited supports The Forest Stewardship
Council® (FSC®), the leading international forest-certification organisation.
Our books carrying the FSC label are printed on FSC®-certified paper.
FSC is the only forest certification scheme supported by the leading
environmental organisations, including Greenpeace. Our paper procurement
policy can be found at: www.randomhouse.co.uk/environment

Printed and bound in Great Britain by Clays Ltd, St Ives PLC

ISBN 9781846043949

Everest illustration by Rodney Paull;
all other illustrations by Gyamtsho Wangdi

Copies are available at special rates for bulk orders. Contact the sales
development team on 020 7840 8487 for more information.

To buy books by your favourite authors and register for offers, visit:
www.randomhouse.co.uk

For the Sherpas of Nepal

❄ CONTENTS

❄ Acknowledgements

Readers may guess that mountaineering, like many fields, has its own inner circle of people who have a long history and maintain close relationships with the climbing fraternity. It was to some of those that we turned for assistance. We remain hugely grateful for their time, generosity and invaluable assistance.

Special thanks go to Lisa Choegyal (Kathmandu) who recorded many of the Sherpa contributions and also to Judy and Tashi Tenzing (Australia) for their invaluable contacts. Thanks also to the renowned Indian mountaineer Captain Mohan Kohli and British climbers Sir Christian Bonington and Doug Scott.

We would also like to thank Liz Hawley (Kathmandu) for running our entries past her impeccable records. For the book's illustrations we are indebted to Gyamtsho Wangdi (Kathmandu), and to Graham Rendoth (Sydney) for drawing the map.

In addition we would like to thank: John Amatt, John Atkin, Barbara Bagnall, Angela Benavides, Arlene Blum, RuthAnn Brown, Michael Brown, Erin Byerly, Jeri Charles, Kevin Cherilla, Jonathan Chester, Greg Child, Katarzyna Cichacka, Paul Deegan, Michael Dillon, Pablo Estevez, Sue Fear, Bruce Gee, Yossi Ghinsberg, Michael Groom, Felipe Guinda, Gary Guller, John Harlin, Rose Janssen, Daniel Koh, Hilary Maitland, Colin Monteath, Ruth Moore, Greg Mortimer, Martin Perelmuter, Marcela Poliacikova, Anna Piunova, Nima Price, Morry Schwartz, Jane Southward, Duncan Thomas, Mike Useem, Amina Waters, Brent Waters, Toby Weare and Minako Yoshida.

We thank Judith Kendra, Publishing Director of Rider at Random House UK, for her boundless enthusiasm, and for ensuring the book's publication in a relatively short time frame. Also at the Random House Base Camp we thank Fiona MacIntyre and our editors for trying to accommodate the voices of over 100 climbers.

❅
FOREWORD
by Doug Scott

Why do people climb mountains? The simple answer for me is I get grumpy when I don't, or I could say because it's in my blood. About two hundred thousand years ago *Homo sapiens* first emerged and began hunting and gathering in small groups for mutual aid. This continued everywhere until the last few thousand years with the urbanisation of the human family.

The chief characteristics of this lengthy period experienced by our ancestors were mainly that they faced uncertainty and risk. To survive in those frugal times they had to be resourceful, imaginative, exploratory and co-operative.

It was not, as Darwin was supposed to have said, the survival of the fittest, but, of course, the survival of the most social. Anthropologists studying remnants of hunter-gathering groups over the last century have detected a common thread inherent in their lifestyle and that is they have to keep in touch with their inner voice. This was easier to access then than now. Life was not one constant quest for the next mouthful of food as our ancestors did have leisure time, probably far more than most of us have now. They had time to paint and carve, and we see from their work that they had the ability to dip below the usual level of consciousness into the subconscious to touch areas of their being that today lie hidden and dormant unless some process is found or some traumatic event occurs to open up.

The universal route towards the inner voice or conscience, which is the same as 'The Great One' of the Naskapi of Labrador or the 'Buddha nature' of the people living around Chomolungma (Everest), is to live harmoniously with the environment and with one's neighbours. This can be equated with climbing where the ultimate tool for survival is intuition or the sixth sense – listening to that inner voice telling you what to do next in the face of approaching storm, potential for avalanche or rock fall, failing strength, disintegrating team effort, homesickness. What chance is there of knowing this sense if you are overwhelmed by ambition and personality conflicts?

In the process of climbing, however, not only do you leave behind every material possession superfluous to actual survival, but also you shed every superfluous thought as you bend to the task of concentrating, hour after hour, day after day, on that next step up.

I know for myself I was very ambitious to climb the southwest face of Everest but, by the time we were above Camp VI, Dougal Haston and I had climbed beyond ego, hardly aware of any expectant public back home, hardly aware of family and friends and, for that matter, hardly aware of each other since we were so focused on each patch of snow, ice or rock. As I warmed to the climb

I experienced a calm prescience that all would be well, it was permissible to maintain upward progress despite steep rock steps and energy-sapping, deep-powder snow. That feeling only comes when everything has a right to be there, when there is the required experience, when a long apprenticeship has been served, when there is patience until everything is right with the mountain and weather and, above all, when the climbers are at peace with themselves and supportive of each other.

Climbing mountains for me has not always worked so well but here it did and, for a time, I was lifted up above my usual state, being more aware of all and everything. It remains a good reference point as to what is possible but it is so hard to hold on to.

INTRODUCTION
by Garry Weare

For trekkers the opportunity to view Everest is a memorable experience. From the ridge above the thriving Sherpa village of Namche Bazaar the summit peers above the massive Lhotse/Nuptse Wall. Yet without the assistance of a guide, few would recognise the summit as being the highest point on earth. It is not until you are practically at the base of Everest that her true dimensions are revealed. Standing atop the nearby peak of Kala Pattar the huge South West flanks of Everest rise the best part of 3,500 metres (11,480 feet) above the Khumbu Glacier. From this perspective many of the classic climbing routes to the summit can be seen and it would be hard to deny that climbing Everest is an awesome achievement.

For the Sherpas, the hardy mountain people who live in the shadow of the world's highest mountain, Everest is also regarded with awe. To them Everest has always been known as Chomolungma the 'Mother Goddess of the World' and is suitably revered in their traditions. Long before they wandered over the high passes from Tibet to settle in Nepal they would have been aware of the mountain's massive size. They would have been familiar with the huge North Face looming at the head of the Rongphu Valley while the Kangshung (East) Face rising high above the verdant Kama Valley would have been equally inspiring.

However, the rest of the world did not know what the Sherpas knew until the later years of the nineteenth century. The Great Trigonometrical Survey of India extended across the entire Indian subcontinent and by 1850 had reached the foothills of the Himalaya. Ascending the ridges above Darjeeling the surveyors would have been struck by the huge dimensions of Kangchenjunga before turning their attention to a distant snow-capped peak on the western horizon. In 1852 they calculated that it was not just higher than Kangchenjunga but was in fact the highest mountain in the world. Its height was calculated at 8,850 metres, 29,035 feet (a remarkable calculation that corresponds exactly to the currently recognised height). At the time the mountain was referred to as Peak 15 and it was only during the final stages of the survey in 1865 that the Royal Geographic Society accepted the proposal to name the peak after the notable Surveyor-General, Sir George Everest.

The discovery of the height of Everest would have made no difference to the Sherpa people. Their life centred on planting their crops of barley, grazing their yaks on the alpine pastures and trading across the nearby border between Nepal and Tibet. They had little idea how Chomolungma would impact on the lives of future generations of Sherpas.

For foreigners the location of Everest – straddling the border between Nepal and Tibet – made it beyond their reach. The kingdom of Nepal guarded its borders carefully and permission would not be granted to travel to Tibet. It was a situation that would continue well into the twentieth century and it was not until the 13th Dalai Lama granted the British authorities in India permission to enter Tibet that the first concerted forays were allowed to explore the lower flanks of Everest.

In the autumn of 1921 the first British reconnaissance team reached the Rongphu Monastery. It was, to use the words of one of the team members, 'an unexpected place of joy'. The letters of introduction from the Dalai Lama ensured that the team was treated as honoured guests. Yet within the confines of the monastery the high lamas held reservations that the sahibs might unwarily upset the gods that resided in the high mountains.

The reconnaissance team lost little time exploring the glaciers and snowfields beneath the summit of Everest. After a series of high altitude forays they decided that the North Col route provided the key to reaching the summit. With this in mind they returned home to plan the first climbing expedition for the following spring.

The 1922 expedition captured the imagination of the British public. After recruiting a team of Sherpas from Darjeeling they embarked on the climb that put them within 500 metres (1,640 feet) of the summit. The expedition exacted a huge cost, with six Sherpas tragically killed in an avalanche below the North Col.

In 1924 another expedition was mounted; two of the strongest climbers, George Mallory and Andrew Irvine, were last seen on the summit ridge 'going strong for the top'. At the time there was much speculation as to whether they did succeed in climbing Everest and it was not until 1999 that an expedition found Mallory's body. However, they were unable to locate his camera which would have solved the dispute beyond doubt.

In 1933 the British returned and were again defeated a short distance below the summit. Yet by now the Himalayan mountaineering culture was changing. In contrast to the large military-style expeditions on Everest, small lightweight expeditions were being undertaken elsewhere in the Himalaya by the likes of Eric Shipton, H.W. Tilman and Frank Smythe. A similar approach was advocated for Everest, although most circles of opinion thought it either logistically impossible or far too ambitious.

Attitudes to the Sherpas were also changing. In the early expeditions the Sherpas were considered at best as high-altitude porters, indispensable in their load-carrying efforts but without the technical climbing expertise to accompany a summit bid. It was not until the 1936 expedition that the British sought their true potential as 'climbing Sherpas'. Whilst the expedition was defeated by an early onset of the monsoon, the Sherpa team did include a young recruit by the name of Tenzing Norgay.

The closing of the Tibetan borders by China in 1949 put a halt to further attempts on Everest. However, in 1950 the King of Nepal granted permission for foreign expeditions to enter the kingdom. Reconnaissance expeditions were mounted in 1950 and in 1951 and the route through the formidable Khumbu Icefall to the South Col was considered as the most likely route to the summit. It was the Swiss who secured the climbing permission on Everest in 1952, with Raymond Lambert and Tenzing Norgay climbing high on the South East Ridge to within sight of the summit. The following year the British expedition led by Colonel John Hunt succeeded. On 29 May 1953, Edmund Hillary and Tenzing Norgay set foot on the highest point on earth.

Since 1953 around 1,500 people have climbed Everest. While most ascents have been made either by the legendary Sherpas or by climbers from countries with strong alpine traditions, other not so obvious countries also figure. Everest has been scaled by climbers from Singapore, Malaysia, Venezuela, Mexico and Ecuador as well as by more than a handful of Australian mountaineers.

As far as the records go, Junko Tabei from Japan was the first woman to summit Everest, in 1975, while Apa Sherpa has summited Everest 21 times. When British mountaineer Chris Bonington (at 50) climbed Everest in 1985 he was for a short period the oldest to reach the summit. At present the oldest is a 76-year-old Nepalese man, Bahadur Sherchan, while the youngest person to summit is Temba Tsheri Sherpa at the tender age of 16.

There has been an upsurge in the numbers climbing Everest over the last decade, but no ascent is straight-forward or easy. The summit of Everest is still subject to huge storms and ferocious winds, while its height and the amount of oxygen on its upper flanks are the same as they were in 1953.

Nowadays few Everest expeditions attract worldwide attention. Yet there still remains a universal curiosity as to why people continue to strive to summit Everest and whether it changes their attitude to life.

Reading the contributions in this book it is evident that to summit Everest demands incredible qualities of courage, determination and physical prowess. As each climber ascends out of the night into the rays of dawn lighting the upper ridges of the mountain, supreme efforts are translated into untold feelings of vision, joy and relief at reaching the summit. There are few whose perspectives do not change, not just on their climbing achievements but about themselves, their future and how they see the world below.

It may be possible to compare the mountaineers' experience of Everest with many of life's other challenges. Indeed, it may also help us to provide a new perspective on our own aspirations and inspire us to strive for our own Everest.

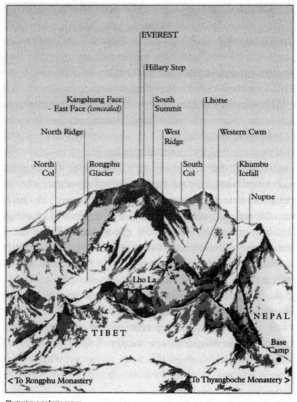

EVEREST

Hillary Step

Kangshung Face
– East Face *(concealed)*

South
Summit

Lhotse

North Ridge

West
Ridge

Western Cwm

North
Col

Rongphu
Glacier

South
Col

Khumbu
Icefall

Nuptse

Lho La

NEPAL

TIBET

Base
Camp

< To Rongphu Monastery

To Thyangboche Monastery >

Illustration: renodesign.com.au

EVEREST
Reflections From The Top

MAJOR (ret.) H. P. S. AHLUWALIA

As a member of the first successful Indian Everest expedition he put a record-breaking nine climbers on the summit on 29 May 1965.

The dominant emotion that surged through me as I stood on the summit of Everest was humility. I felt, 'Thank God, it's all over,' but instead of jubilation, there was a tinge of sadness. Was it because I had done the ultimate in climbing and all roads hereafter would lead down?

In climbing to the summit you are overwhelmed by a deep sense of joy and thankfulness which lasts a lifetime, and the experience changes you completely. The man who has been to the mountains is never the same again; he becomes conscious of his smallness and loneliness in the universe.

That other summit – the summit of the mind – is no less formidable and no easier to climb.

The mind has its mountains and cliffs, fearful, sheer, unfathomed. The physical act of climbing a mountain has a kinship with the ascent of that inward, spiritual mountain.

STACY ALLISON

The first American woman to climb Everest reached the summit on 29 September 1988.

The summit experience was ephemeral and gone in an hour. Now I have to think hard to remember what it felt like up there.

But the climb itself is in the marrow of my bones, like all the other climbs, adventures and experiences in my life.

It's in the friends I made, what I learned about myself when I failed on my first attempt, and what I proved when I dusted myself off and went back to try again. The summit was a dream, but when I was climbing, I was as wide awake and open to experience as I have ever been. Everest is behind me now, but I can still see her shadow in everything I do. It's a reminder, a challenge, from the highest spot on earth: Look beyond the ordinary. There's always something more. As long as I remember that, I know anything is possible.

ANG JANGBU SHERPA

Born in Pangboche, Nepal, he is known locally as 'Legs Ang Jangbu' for his remarkable physique. He reached the summit on 2 October 1979 with the Swabian Everest expedition on which Ray Genet and Hannelore Schmatz perished. He now lives in Kathmandu.

It was a childhood ambition to climb Sagarmatha [Everest]. Now I am old and fat and smoke. It was very late when we reached the summit and I had wanted to turn back earlier as two members of the team were very weak. My Sherpa partner Sungdare and I gave them our oxygen. Below the South Summit it was getting dark and they wanted to stop. I got angry. 'You cannot stay so high. You must listen to us, this is our Sagarmatha not Mount McKinley.'

They insisted on bivouacking. I did not want to lose fingers or toes, or die. I left my pack and oxygen with them, and started down alone. There was no moon but the night was thick with stars. When I reached the South Col I was so tired I got into the sleeping bag with my boots on. Next morning, after a cup of soup I had a good feeling to be alive. I watched the others, first two moving down, then only one. Sungdare got frostbite but he was the only one to come back.

ANG PHURBA SHERPA

A mountaineer, a social worker and a prominent leader of the Khumbu community, Ang Phurba Sherpa comes from Namche Bazaar in Nepal. He summited Everest on 2 October 1979.

I was the only Sherpa with three team members roped together. I did not know the way but just kept going upwards. It was windy and snowy and hard to see. As we got near the top I asked the team to wait and I went ahead as I had some trouble finding the route.

Visibility was so bad, I only realised I was on the summit when my foot knocked against the metal tripod. I yelled to my team, 'This is the summit. Come up!' Even though they did not all speak English, I could tell they were happy and excited. We took some pictures, and I felt I would like to climb from other routes, set new records and climb Sagarmatha many times.

The whole nation grieved at the loss of our world-famous Babu Chhiri Sherpa on 29 April 2001 after 10 Everest summits. He also held the record of spending the longest time on the summit – more than 21 hours. I was at base camp and paid tribute to his body. I thought how cruel and heartless the crevasses are which had to carry away Babu. It seemed as if nature also mourned as it started snowing lightly, the air was still, the sky was all cloudy and a black shroud engulfed the mountain.

CONRAD ANKER

The American adventurer and climber summited Everest on 17 May 1999. As one of the team searching for the famous lost British mountaineers George Mallory and Andrew Irvine, he came across the body of George Mallory at approx. 8,230 metres (27,000 feet) on the North Face of Everest on 3 May 1999.

Making it to the summit was not what I had imagined it would be. I thought the view would be similar to the panoramic tourist posters in Kathmandu and the moment would be one of great elation. It was not like that. It was damn cold and an eerie fog drifted between us and the sky above. My climbing partner Dave Hahn and I snapped a picture of each other on this most significant, yet at the time seemingly nondescript, bit of our planet. The enjoyment of having made it to the top is greater now than it was at three in the afternoon on the day I summited.

APA SHERPA

This Nepalese climber made his twenty-first Everest summit in May 2011.

I have never felt afraid on Everest. Climbing on this mountain for me is like a child climbing on to its mother's lap. I have full trust in her but I try not to make her angry or show disrespect. She has always shown me kindness and allowed me to climb safely and I am very grateful. But she has told me that it is enough now and I behave as an obedient child towards her.

STEVE BELL

The proprietor of a leading mountaineering company, he was the first Briton to lead paying clients to the summit of Everest, having summited the mountain on 7 October 1993.

Many Everest summiteers divide their lives into two halves, life before and life after Everest. Fear has been a major emotion on all of my Everest trips: fear that I might die, fear that I might fail. There was even fear that I would succeed, because of how that might change my life.

Now that I have been there, its secret has gone, and the fear and uncertainty of what life after Everest might hold has gone with it. But it was a thrilling sensation to be up there on the summit, crossing the gulf between life before and life after, and knowing that I would never be able to return.

WILLIE BENEGAS

This Argentinian climber who now lives in California summited Everest three times, in 1999, 2001 and 2002.

Everest belongs to the Sherpas and when we summit they allow us to take a peek at their special place.

Everest either gives you permission to climb or not and decides if you will live or die at the summit. After you have summited it affects you at a very deep level, and gives you a wake-up call to think about how you relate to people and to yourself.

At the summit I saw and felt the presence of my late father and he gave me the energy to descend safely. Each time I have also felt that my twin brother Damian was by my side.

I believe that if you respect Everest, and take care of it, the mountain will take care of you.

LUIS BENITEZ

Born in Ecuador but now living in the United States, he summited Everest on 25 May 2001 when he guided Erik Weihenmayer to the summit.

I started dreaming of Everest as a child when my asthma and allergies were so terrible that I had to fight to breathe even at sea level.

When I first went to Everest, it was with a blind man who wanted to tell the world the same things that I believed in: that there are no boundaries except the self-imposed ones, and that the mind can push the body beyond what it thought was possible. As we walked arm in arm to the roof of the world, I realised that one must inspire the next generation always to push beyond those limiting boundaries.

EUGENE BERGER

This former teacher and alpine guide was Minister for the Environment in Luxembourg from 1999 to 2004. He summited Everest on 1 October 1992.

Everest is an intensely personal challenge. How far can you push your own limits mentally and physically?

Finally the top delivers you and it is magical how some icy square metres of snow high up in the thin air suddenly turn you upside down. When you put your feet on them it's as if you are beamed into a new life, completely fulfilled and at the same time lost because your dreams are suddenly empty again.

❊
EVELYNE BINSACK

After amassing an impressive climbing record in the European Alps, she was the first Swiss woman to summit Everest, on 23 May 2001.

Alpinism for women is very hard. But I yearned to climb Everest, to do something for myself, without male competition.

As I reached base camp in Tibet I felt very meek and knew that if I summited Chomolungma it would change my life. When I recall the experience it gives me a feeling of inner power and smooths the way for my vision of helping people with my skill as an Alpine helicopter pilot.

ROMAN BLANCO

When he summited on 7 October 1993, this Spanish climber was the oldest (at the age of 60) to climb Everest.

After crossing the Khumbu Icefall and reaching Camp 2 at the Western Cwm I was already shedding tears of emotion. It seemed impossible for me to actually be there. I was very satisfied to reach that level, and accepted I might not be able to attempt the summit. But summit I did. I remember whispering, 'I made it!'

The tears came back and the immense and grandiose solitude of the mountains became embedded in my memory for ever.

ALEXEI BOLOTOV

On 18 May 1998, Russian mountaineer Alexei Bolotov summited Everest.

I have been to Everest twice, and the second time was without oxygen. I was happy and filled with emotion, because for me, as for all summiteers, Everest is no ordinary mountain. It is a symbol, a dream – and that dream came true for me.

CHRIS BONINGTON

A legend in British mountaineering history, he has achieved a string of first ascents and has been expedition leader on many celebrated Himalayan climbs, including the Everest South West Face Expedition (1975). He first summited Everest on 21 April 1985 on an expedition led by the Norwegian adventurer Arne Naess.

I had mixed feelings as I struggled those last few feet to the top of Everest. I couldn't help thinking of the all too many climbing friends who had lost their lives in the last few years. Four of our summit team were already there when I got to the top. I just slumped into the snow and cried. They were tears of grief for lost friends, of sheer exhaustion and joy that I had finally made it – and that Pertemba, who had been my sirdar on the South West Face in 1975, was there, for the third time, to share my experience, as well as two good new friends, Bjorn Myrer-Lund and Odd Eliassen.

Slowly I became aware of where I was. It was a superb day with hardly a cloud in the sky. I gazed down the North East Ridge and to the Rongphu Glacier far below. To the north, the Tibetan plateau stretched into the far distance, rolling hills like a brown ocean with the occasional white cap of a distant peak. To the south, now far below me, was the summit of Nuptse, which I had climbed all those years ago, while to the west and east stretched the chain of the Himalaya. The team hugged, I took some pictures and after about half an hour on the summit we started back down.

Everest is the only peak I've climbed in the world's greatest ranges that wasn't a first ascent or by a new route. We climbed the trade route, and I think it was about the 250th ascent. For a few days I was the oldest, at 50, to have climbed Everest. That in itself is no big deal. The climb meant, and still does mean, a huge amount to me. It was partly the nature of the experience. The Norwegians were a great crowd and it had been a very happy expedition. It was just having been there, and enjoying that view as I stood on the highest point on earth. It was immensely fulfilling and the end of an era, after all those earlier expeditions to the South West Face of Everest and its grim North Ridge.

❆
STIPE BOZIC

Croatia's most accomplished climber and adventure film-maker summited Everest on 15 May 1979 and again on 10 May 1989. He has climbed all Seven Summits.

I had good luck on the steep way to Everest's throne, which drew me up there with its magical powers. My health was good and I did not have any conflict with my fellow climbers.

May 15,1979 dawned a beautiful day and it was the happiest day of my life. It changed everything and I felt as if I was an ambassador for all my friends and everyone else in the world who ever dreamed of summiting Everest. Up there a man rarely wins, and he can also die. I think climbers are a little crazy to tackle something so challenging, but generally not so crazy that they allow themselves to come to grief. God, oh how happy I am to be alive!

❄ LYDIA BRADEY

On 14 October 1988 she became the first woman to climb Everest without oxygen, and the first New Zealand woman to summit.

I remember sitting at Camp 3 (7,300 metres; 23,950 feet) and endlessly looking at the top slopes almost bursting with curiosity as to what it might be like *up there*. What would it be like to be so high, to breathe on top, and what will the view be like on the other side?

I spent maybe 10 minutes on the main summit and it was all fantastic, and it was fantastic all day. What impressed me the most was the sensation of climbing on such a huge massif, just being on such a large piece of earth, with its wings and drops and cliffs and ice slopes sweeping away from you in different directions.

✿
MICHAEL BROWN

After summiting Everest on 22 May 2000, the American adventure filmmaker returned and summited again on 25 May 2001 when filming Erik Weihenmayer's ascent.

I asked myself, 'Could I do that?' Everest became my secret ambition.

Two years later I experienced that huge summit day first hand. Climbing through the night looking up at the stars clustered around the south summit was a sublime other-worldly experience. My three Sherpa friends Khami, Tashi and Phu Tashi took me under their wing, and we eventually made it to the summit. I was taking some images and contemplating the descent – then it hit me, and tears welled up unexpectedly.

I had an enormous feeling of happiness and satisfaction. Little, insecure, non-athletic geek was standing on the top of the world.

Nothing has been the same since that day. I don't walk up to people and say, 'Hi, I climbed Everest,' because it doesn't really matter if anyone knows. It is part of my history that is measurable in everyone's terms, but most importantly my own.

SHERMAN BULL

A physician and for a time the oldest person to climb Everest, he summited on 25 May 2001 at the age of 64. Sherman is one of the oldest people to have climbed all Seven Summits. His son Brad had previously summited on 15 May 1995.

At 64 years of age, on my fifth attempt, I finally stood on top of the world with my son, Brad. Our team was spearheaded by Erik Weihenmayer, a spectacular mountaineer by any standards, who happens to be blind. We climbed through a major storm at the Balcony and almost turned back at 2 a.m. However, due to good radio contact with our support team, we persisted and the crimson dawn ushered in a perfect summit day. One can imagine the flood of emotions as 19 of our 21-member team stood on the summit, including the blind climber and the father-son duo. None of us will ever forget it.

✳
ADRIAN BURGESS

This British mountaineer, now resident in the USA, summited Everest on 24 May 1989.

I arrived on the summit at 7 a.m., just as the sun, rising out of Tibet, projected the mountain's dark form across the low-lying clouds of Nepal. My companions, Ang Lakpa, Sonam Dendu and Roddy Mackenzie, had left the South Col at midnight during perfect weather. I am often asked what it feels like to be standing on the highest part of the planet.

Ang Lakpa had some small tissue notelets with Buddhist prayers printed upon them. He handed some to me and told me to throw them up into the air in honour of the gods. They hung there, caught in the updraughts about 6 metres (20 feet) above our heads. So when I was on the summit I was looking up, not down, and all I could think was: Yes, I am on the highest point – but there is a heck of a lot more up there.

✱
DUNCAN CHESSELL

Australian mountain guide and geologist Duncan Chessell summited Everest on 23 May 2001.

The summit takes a while to sink in, but before that could happen Mark Auricht died of a stroke below Camp 2 on the descent.

Celebrating the climb stopped and it wasn't until six months or more later that I actually felt happy at all about the team's success. It will always be tainted by Mark's death and the disappointment of his failure to summit when we had both worked so hard to get there.

CHHULDIM DORJE SHERPA

Known as Ang Dorje Sherpa and originally from Pangboche in the Everest region of Nepal, he has reached Everest's summit ten times, mostly working as a senior guide on New Zealand corporate climbing expeditions.

I was so happy the first time I reached the summit. Sometimes I am scared about getting myself and the members of my team down safely. Some are not fit, experienced or so strong.

When I am on the summit sometimes I worry I am stepping on my god Sagarmatha. Only twice has it been clear on top. From the Tibet side you can see many blue lakes, brown plateaux and some white peaks. The Nepal side is all ridges criss-crossing each other. You cannot imagine how beautiful.

GREG CHILD

As well as being a distinguished Himalaya climber who summited Everest on 26 May 1995, this Australian mountaineer has received numerous awards for mountain writing. He now lives in the USA.

I had always sneered at Everest, and snubbed invitations to go on expeditions to it: I thought it was an overrated, over-climbed status symbol. But in 1995 I went to the mountain maybe because I was tired of making excuses as to why I had climbed so many Himalayan peaks, but not Everest.

Whatever the reason, as the departure date for Tibet neared, I did feel a growing fascination. Perhaps it was a dose of Everest fever. Mostly, though, I just wanted to get the mountain off my back.

I justified selling out my 'no-Everest' principles because I had a project up there: to make a film about climbing the North Ridge with an old friend Tom Whittaker who is an amputee. I resolved to help him become the first amputee up Everest. 'Why would I want to climb with a one-legged man, Tom?' I asked him bluntly. 'Because it will make us both very sexy,' he replied.

The sun was rising when we hit the ridge crest and Tibet's horizon was a sheet of earth-coloured velvet, the foreground a swirl of porcelain-white glaciers.

The summit proved to be a busy spot. For the seven of us up there, there were hands to shake, radio broadcasts to make and photos to take. I remembered that in 1990 on K2 I hallucinated and saw the figure of a person. On Everest, on that summit day, not seeing a person constituted an hallucination.

I spent a few minutes on top alone. Quiet at last. Just the flapping prayer flags and the beat and heave of my heart and lungs. No clouds. A curving horizon.

Somewhere out there in the great southern distance the monsoon was rolling towards the Himalaya, pushing aside the jet-stream winds like a cosmic bulldozer to create the freakish spell of calm that surrounded Everest. Record-keepers tell me that mine was the 736th ascent of the mountain. Not exactly an exclusive club, but it felt good to have stood up there.

Tom Whittaker did not summit that year but returned three years later to achieve his goal.

KHOO SWEE CHIOW

On the 25 May 1998 the Singapore adventurer realised his dream to climb Everest when he and Edwin Siew became the first climbers from Singapore to summit.

I first saw Everest in 1989. Nine years later, I stood on its summit. It was a magical and awesome morning.

Having been to the highest point on earth, I saw how I should live my life down in the valley. I needed to be kinder to people, to have an appreciation of God's beautiful creation and to try to preserve what we have for the generations to come.

RENATA CHLUMSKA

The first Swedish woman to climb Everest, on 5 May 1999, she achieved this four years after taking her first climbing course.

I don't think the idea of climbing Everest ever crossed my mind. Not because I thought that I couldn't manage such a challenge, but I believed that climbing Everest was meant only for a few specially chosen people.

Reaching the summit was almost unbelievable, a great adventure.

I still believe that Everest is only for the chosen ones, for those who choose it themselves. Fortunately I am one of them.

GUY COTTER

As one of New Zealand's most accomplished climbers, he has been a defining force in the evolution of guided climbs on Everest. Since first summiting on 12 May 1992 he has returned regularly to Everest, and summited again on 23 May 1997.

Many people ask, 'What is it like on the summit of Everest?' Well, for me the experience was incredible. It was the end of a long and difficult journey. To stand up there and look out over Nepal and Tibet and see the curvature of the earth is spellbinding.

The most rewarding aspect of climbing Everest was the strong friendships I developed with my team mates, Sherpa staff and people from all over the world, all of us sharing a driving passion.

Now when I think about climbing Everest, I have snapshots of the fine times and shared experiences where life is not just being lived, it is coming at you full on.

✳

ANNA CZERWINSKA

On 22 May 2000, when this Polish mountaineer summited Everest, she was the oldest woman at that time to do so, at the age of 51. She has now climbed all Seven Summits.

When I reached the South Summit I looked back at the mists rising from the valleys and I could feel their damp touch on my face. They prevented me from looking down on the long, painful way up, but it was not only that. The curtain of mist had also closed over my past.

My oxygen was running out and common sense demanded that I retreat, but before long I was climbing on an exposed ridge to the foot of the Hillary Step. A crampon had come undone, and I painfully put it on again. Everest was doing everything to discourage me. I registered that dreamily and, as if dreaming, conquered the final metres of the snowy slope.

Suddenly, the clouds above me lifted in one blue moment and, very low down, I saw a rugged, precipitous ridge.

The wind was growing stronger and it was snowing lightly. I did not get the beautiful view as a reward and I felt a bit disappointed.

However, those few minutes on the highest spot on earth were worth every effort.

DAWA TASHI SHERPA

A native of the Beding district of Nepal, Dawa Tashi Sherpa has reached the summit of Everest six times.

I have been on the summit twice without oxygen, but I worry that my mind will become damaged so it is better to use oxygen.

After my sixth summit I thought I would like to go 11 or 12 times, but now I am getting fat so going to high places is a problem. In 1994 I was saved from being swept away in an avalanche by being 2 metres (6.5 feet) up the hill. My cousin was swept away and killed.

I do not want my four daughters to climb. I climb for their education so they can do other business.

RENÉ DE BOS

After he summited Everest on 7 October 1990 the Dutch climber amassed an impressive record of Himalayan ascents.

It was never my intention to climb Everest but once I got the opportunity financially – what a dreadful reason – and became a member of the French expedition I was determined to summit or climb at least as high as I possibly could.

While climbing Everest was not technically my hardest climb, it reaffirmed my belief in the underlying spiritual aspirations of the Buddhists and Hindus of Nepal who gain their inspiration from the Himalaya.

JOSÉ ANTONIO DELGADO

Along with Marcus Tobia, mechanical engineer and mountaineer José Antonio Delgado was the first climber from Venezuela to summit Everest, on 23 May 2001.

We represented the 61st country and were about the 1,000th climbers to reach the top of Everest. We climbed the classical north route in the usual way so it was not a special milestone for the climbing community, but it fulfilled a long-standing dream, and gave hope and happiness to many people in Venezuela.

DICKY DOLMA

On 10 May 1993 this Indian climber became the youngest woman to summit Everest.

I am the youngest woman in the world to summit Everest. I was aged 19 when I got the opportunity to do this as a member of the Indo-Nepalese Women's Everest Expedition in 1993.

It was a dream come true. Not every mountaineer gets the ultimate reward – to summit Everest.

I was worried about returning safely, but by God's grace and sheer determination I succeeded. I belong to a poor family and I had to work very hard to pay all the costs involved.

By climbing Everest I learned one thing: that we are just a small part of Mother Nature.

RALF DUJMOVITS

Since summiting Everest on 4 October 1992 this renowned German mountaineer has led climbs on many other Himalayan expeditions.

I had my whole team up at the South Col, but because of extreme cold and difficult conditions we turned back at the South Summit. Eight days later I returned to the South Col with 10 members.

Strong winds discouraged us again, and everyone except Sonam Tshering Sherpa and myself turned back. We spent a third night at the South Col without oxygen but as the wind continued roaring into the next night Sonam and I decided to climb with oxygen. In horribly stormy conditions, after five hours and 15 minutes, we reached the summit. Sonam died the following spring while descending from the summit, and I lost a very good friend.

Spending the night at 8,000 metres (26,246 feet) before going to the summit is something which affects even the strongest of us, and I fear it will lead to further major disasters on Everest.

JASON EDWARDS

As leader of an international expedition, the American alpine guide summited Everest on 24 May 2001.

I have seen aspiring Everest climbers turn around after just one trip through the Khumbu Icefall and never return to make another attempt at the upper mountain. But many others are willing to risk everything to summit: even their lives.

Quite simply, it's a dangerous place from top to bottom.

Luck and fate are fundamental forces of nature, which act as guardians of a goal that many of us have spent years pursuing.

I have been one of the lucky ones to climb on Everest during four different expeditions, and on my last attempt I finally reached the summit along with 13 other team members. I left the tent each day and asked myself the critical question, 'Do I feel lucky today?' Then I would start back up the mountain again, and quietly say my prayers and hope I would indeed be lucky today. The rest is history.

SUSAN AND PHIL ERSHLER

Having first summited Everest on 20 October 1984, the American climber Phil Ershler returned 18 years later. This time he summited with his wife, Susan, on 16 May 2002. They are the first married couple to have climbed all Seven Summits.

I was motivated to climb Everest because Phil and I had set out on a journey with the objective of climbing all Seven Summits together. Our feeling at the top of Everest was of overwhelming happiness that we were able to share our success.

NANCY FEAGIN

The experienced American Big Wall climber summited Everest on 24 May 2001.

I have focused on highly technical climbing at relatively low altitudes for over 20 years and was intrigued by the idea of climbing at such a high altitude and experiencing Everest first hand.

I felt so small and insignificant in relation to my surroundings. It was like being in a dream. We were all moving about slowly and methodically. I'm sure the lack of oxygen enhanced my dreamlike state. The months of preparation, the journey, the climb had now been accomplished. My mother spoke to me from base camp. 'Nancy, we're so proud of you. Now be careful on the way down.' The fear in her voice jolted me back to reality. 'Yes, Mom . . . I'll be careful . . . I love you.' It didn't sink in for quite some time that we had succeeded.

The climb made me realise how important my family and friends are to me and the Sherpas captured a special place in my heart. Their generosity, hard work and dedication are incredible. Their easy laugh made it truly a joy to be in their community.

SVEN GANGDAL

*After two unsuccessful attempts this Norwegian mountaineer
fulfilled his ambition to summit Everest on 17 May 1996.*

We didn't cry or shout, we didn't get that kick. The success and crying was definitely inside us, and still I feel ambivalence about my ascent of Everest.

I read about Sir Edmund Hillary's conquest of Everest when I was a kid. In stark contrast, my second attempt on the mountain ended with the death of my friend Mingma Norbu Sherpa on the West Ridge in 1994. I reached my ultimate mountaineering goal by the North Ridge on the morning of Norwegian National Day. My climbing partners Olav Storli Ulvund, Dawa Tsering Sherpa, Dawa Tashi Sherpa and I had lots of energy and powered all the way up.

The climb and the summit were fantastic but there are enormous paradoxes to come to terms with. Stepping over bodies of friends on the way up, and losing our Austrian friend at the highest camp when we were descending and so close to celebrating our success. The simple question is: 'How desperate can people be to reach the summit of Everest?' The answer is unfortunately simple too: 'There are no limits.'

MICHAEL GROOM

After seriously damaging both feet on Kangchenjunga in 1986, the Australian climber had to learn to walk again. Three years later he set out to climb 'the Big Five' 8,000 metre (26,246 feet) peaks and summited Everest on 10 May 1993 and 10 May 1996.

I wanted to climb Everest from the time I started school. My classmates laughed at me for harbouring such an unusual ambition. For years I succumbed to peer pressure and played more acceptable sports, but deep down I knew I would become a climber.

I spent 13 years doing my Himalayan apprenticeship and finally, at 10.20 a.m. on 10 May 1993, the summit of Everest was where I was standing, alone. It was the only time in my life when I felt that I was *really there*.

After two failed expeditions to Everest, one of which resulted in a 900-metre (2,950-feet) fall down the Lhotse Face in an avalanche, plus having to learn how to walk again after the loss of 30 per cent of both feet, due to frostbite on Kangchenjunga, I couldn't quite believe I had made it.

I slapped my face to make sure it was not just another dream.

BEAR GRYLLS

Former British SAS soldier and author, he became the youngest British mountaineer to climb Everest when he summited on 26 May 1998.

As a kid I spent hours staring intently at a picture my late father had given me of the icy faces of Everest. I lay in the dark and warmth of my room trying desperately to imagine what it would be like to be alone up there, in the cold winds that roll across her face. As my father taught me to climb on tiny mountain faces, these images of Everest stayed with me. My father gave action to my dream, and in life that makes all the difference.

When I broke my back parachuting while serving with the British Special Forces, that dream to attempt Everest died. I could hardly move and was struggling even to sit up in bed. The pictures of Everest now only upset me. But as I began to recover slowly they also gave me hope, and hope keeps people alive, especially on mountains.

High mountains have a way of binding people together but I found it was my father's spirit and my faith in the Almighty that helped me up high when all reason and physical strength seemed far away. During those long nights of climbing, cold and frightened, I would often remember this one verse from Psalm 121:

I lift mine eyes up to the mountain, where does my help come from? My help comes from you, Maker of heaven, creator of the earth.

You find that any romance falls away pretty quickly, especially at minus 30 degrees Celsius, but I did feel a presence on the summit in a way I had never known before.

I just wish I could have bottled that moment, but maybe it is simply that which makes this mountain so intensely special.

BERNARDO GUARACHI

On 25 May 1998 this mountaineer and Aymara Indian became the only Bolivian to summit Everest. A commemorative stamp was released to celebrate his achievement.

After reaching the top of Sagarmatha I promised myself that I would relate more strongly to nature and other human beings. I had very strong feelings about summiting for at least two months, and then I gradually settled down.

HELGA HENGGE

New York-based fashion stylist and German/American climber, she summited Everest on 27 May 1999.

Never will I forget the night we climbed to the top of the world, and joined the full moon, which lit up thousands of tiny snow crystals and called them forth to dance into the heavens.

I was surprised how fast we reached the North East Ridge and in wonder I crouched low and pressed my down jacket into the frozen snowdrift. Then I slowly inched forward to look out over the Kangshung Face. The mountain seemed to emit a pure white light, which illuminated the night. Vast snowfields fell away into unknown depths and millions of stars glistened before us. The night was strangely still, and in the stillness all around I felt I could hear the fluttering of angels' wings.

We had stepped out of life long ago and entered the heavenly spheres, and for an eternal moment I stopped living and started being.

That night the moon danced so gloriously in heaven, the eternal light which touches our world calling all beings forth to dance with great compassion. This is the home of the gods – the great Himalaya.

PETER HILLARY

On 10 May 1990, 37 years after his father Sir Edmund Hillary, he became the first son of an Everest summiteer to repeat the achievement. He returned to Everest and summited again on 25 May 2002. Peter is also a founding director of the Australian Himalayan Foundation.

For the Hillary family Everest has been a defining event, as we have climbed upon it and built schools and hospitals around the foot of it for the local people.

The expeditionary experience of climbing Everest, and surviving it, has changed our lives.

To push yourself to within a wisp of life itself and return to the world in the valleys below is to see life in its raw immediacy and in its essential components. This stark contrast to our other life is a lesson learned and a personal triumph to carry with you every day.

My two summits of this greatest of mountains are defining moments for me yet they pale into insignificance beside the climb of my father and Tenzing in 1953. They climbed what was thought to be unclimbable; they ascended to an altitude beyond what was thought was possible for humans; they broke through a barrier and so established a new standard for all of us to follow. Fifty years on and the mountain hasn't changed. It is we who have been changed.

AL HINKES

This British climber summited Everest on 19 May 1996 via the North Col and North East Ridge. He has now climbed all 14 8,000-metre (26,246 feet) peaks.

I felt privileged to be on top of the world. A strange feeling of 'You'd better believe this, Alan, you've finally bagged Everest, now get down.' I took out photographs of my Gran and daughter Fiona for my summit picture. I usually take a photo of Fiona to the top rather than the nation's flag.

I only stayed on top for 15 or 20 minutes before focusing my mind on the descent. Fiona would want her dad back and Gran would want me back too. No mountain, not even Everest, is worth a life. Returning is a success, the summit only a bonus.

❄

SKIP HORNER

When this American climber summited Everest on 12 May 1992, he became the first to have guided all Seven Summits.

Climbing Everest was for me the ultimate personal goal and the ultimate team effort.

We suffer alone up there. That inner voice keeps us motivated and focused, and our pain and turmoil is quite personal. As a guide I also had to motivate the man at the other end of the rope, for whom I was responsible, and for whom I also had to suffer some pain and resolve some turmoil.

In addition we climbed for the rest of the team, who had worked so hard to give us this chance. I think of Everest, and of guiding the Seven Summits, every day of my life, and it continues to give me deep satisfaction.

CRAIG JOHN

Highly regarded American mountain guide, he summited Everest on 25 May 1998.

I had my best day in the mountains that day and I had it when I needed it. It was intense but immensely satisfying. We crossed the Triangle Snowfield just below the summit and crossed over to the North Face. I looked up the gully we had to ascend and thought that it would take for ever.

Ten minutes later I could see my friend Lhakpa on the summit and five minutes of walking on the most beautiful ridge I had ever seen took me there. For a minute I couldn't speak. I was choked with emotion. I thought of my late climbing friend Mike Rheinberger who had perished on Everest in 1994, and Mark Whetu and the other friends who had been here before me.

I was lucky to live my biggest dream. Fifteen minutes later I thought of the business at hand – getting down.

RODRIGO JORDAN

Heralded by Time *magazine in 1995 as one of the leaders of the 'new millennium', this Oxford University graduate and Chilean climber summited via the Kangshung Face of Everest on 15 May 1992.*

On the summit of Everest, my climbing partner Cristián García-Huidobro took a picture of the footprints he left on the snow as he approached it. The steps of only one climber but the result of the collective effort of many.

Is it the summit of Everest which really matters?

To me what really matters are the people with whom I climb: the climbers with whom I share the extreme experience of attempting Everest. They help you become more understanding and tolerant. The human experience is the highest reward in deep adventure.

While on the summit of Everest I sensed the uttermost expression of the collaborative art of mountaineering.

ERLING KAGGE

As well as summiting Everest on 9 May 1996, Norwegian Erling Kagge is a world-renowned adventurer, the first person to travel solo to the South Pole, and the first to reach the three Poles (Everest, North and South Poles) by land.

We are all explorers of our own lives, whatever path we take. There is nothing rational about what I have done. Skiing to the Poles, sailing the oceans and climbing Everest. These are absurd undertakings, which do not contribute to improving the environment or world peace.

However, every summiting of Everest is a positive contribution because it reminds people of the grandeur of nature and is a genuine invitation to everybody to find their own Everest within.

✳

KAJI SHERPA

With his speed ascent of Everest (20 hours and 24 minutes from base camp to summit), Kaji Sherpa from the Solu Khumbu region of Nepal made the Guinness Book of Records *in 1998. Between 1992 and 1998 he climbed Everest five times.*

On the summit I am always very relaxed and happy. I want to go again very fast and break the record. My most bitter experience on Everest was when some of my friends lost their lives in front of my eyes from a fall at 7,000 metres (22,965 feet) on the Tibetan side in 1995. It grieved and shocked me very much, and I considered abandoning this profession for ever.

DAVO KARNICAR

The Slovenian climber and skier who summited Everest on
7 October 2000 and skied back to base camp later that day!

I devoted myself to Everest for five years after my brother
Andrej and I were the first people to ski off Annapurna
(8,091 metres; 26,545 feet). In 1996 I tried to climb
Everest from the north side, but the weather deterio-
rated and I lost two fingers on my left hand.

I realised that the only way to ski continuously from
Everest was from the same direction as the first summiteers. I had met Mr Hillary and this strongly influenced
my decision, because he did not negate the possibility of
skiing from the top.

At the summit I exchanged my climbing equipment
for the skiing equipment that I had carried up myself. I
was happy, because I was aware that on Everest a man
was the furthest away from the corruption of the mod-
ern world. I embraced the idea of all the beautiful things
which life offered.

The 20-metre-/65.5 feet-long wavy ridge above the
Hillary Step was technically the most difficult part to
ski. The Step itself was heavily covered in snow, since it
was the post-monsoon period.

Skiing between the Icefall and Everest's west shoulder presented the biggest mental challenge. There was the constant threat of falling seracs and avalanches. Skiing 3,500 metres (11,483 feet) of difference in height took four hours and 40 minutes, including rest stops from the highest spot to the last snowfield at the foothills.

TEODORS KIRSIS

Leader of the first two Latvian Himalayan expeditions, Professor Teodors Kirsis summited Everest on 14 May 1995.

Wandering between the sky and the earth below I didn't really know or ask myself why I was there.

When we were moving on the hard snow of the summit pyramid, our minds still refused to accept it was the snow of Everest.

It was like walking into a dream, touching a rainbow and brushing with the eternal legends of climbing. Forgetting about oxygen, for 45 minutes on top of the world we were doing all those funny things people do on top of a mountain, and we were happy. I am not a superstitious man, but before leaving I turned and thanked the mountain for letting us come, climb and leave it as free men.

KARI KOBLER

This Swiss mountaineer led an international expedition on Everest when he summited on 17 May 2000.

When I finally climbed Everest the weather was very good and it honestly felt like climbing Rauflihorn (a small mountain in Switzerland). Summiting Everest did not have a direct effect on me personally but many people had quite a strong – mostly positive – reaction to this achievement.

GORAN KROPP

One of Sweden's most celebrated adventurers, he is best known for cycling 11,265 kilometres (7,000 miles) from his former home in Sweden to Everest, climbing the mountain without oxygen and returning by bicycle to Sweden. He summited Everest on 23 May 1996 and 5 May 1999.

Tragically, Goran died in a climbing accident near his new home base of Washington, USA on 30 September 2002.

My motivation to climb Everest was that I wanted to do so without any assistance, all the way from my home to the summit and back again. The moment when I reached the summit for the first time was not all filled with joy.

I felt that I had been stretched to my limit and touched the border between life and death. I was afraid to end like the other climbers who had died in a storm two weeks earlier. It was not until I reached the safety of base camp that I felt overwhelming happiness and confidence. 'Goran, you can do something seemingly impossible if you prepare yourself carefully and are willing to give 100 per cent.' My next goal is Antarctica – here I come!

BRONCO LANE

As a member of the British Army expedition in 1976, he was among the first handful of British climbers to summit Everest. He summited on 16 May 1976.

Our team had no prima donnas, and unselfishness was displayed to a very high degree. Unfortunately we lost Terry Thompson in a tragic accident, which marred our ascent. Losing a climbing companion is a stark reminder that you do not *conquer* mountains, but sneak up and down when nature has her back turned. While returning from the summit my climbing partner Brummie Stokes and I were benighted at 8,535 metres (28,000 feet) and bivouacked without protection. Both of us lost all our toes and some fingertips.

NEIL LAUGHTON

This British climber has completed the Seven Summits. He climbed Everest on 26 May 1998.

It was a tough decision to return to Everest, given my painful memories of being caught at 8,000 metres (26,246 feet) in the fatal storm of 1996.

We did well to get to the South Summit but one of my colleagues needed help to get back down to base camp. Once safely there, after a big meal and a few hours' sleep I was heading back up to the top again. To stand on the summit with freezing toes on the anniversary of my father's death was the most memorable experience of my life. I said a prayer of thanks and my thoughts turned to those who had lost their lives in pursuit of that glorious view.

DOLLY LEFEVER

An American climber, based in Alaska, she first attempted Everest in 1989. She returned and summited on 10 May 1993.

I cannot explain the relentless drive to climb majestic mountains. It's probably insanity. On my summit bid, I had a defective oxygen bottle and I finally ran out of air high up on Everest. It felt like someone was sucking all the air out of me before it reached my lungs.

I was travelling in a whiteout in a new snowfall when I tripped on my crampon. I fell head over heels and my ice axe had no bite in the new snow over icy slate rock. I had no idea if I would live or die in the minutes until I finally arrested my fall. Some greater being had more plans for my life here.

I came away from Everest knowing that the Mother Goddess was looking out for me that day. I also found out that I wanted to make changes in how I related to myself and the people I share my world with. Life is precious. We all find ways to explore self and life but in the end all this activity is about learning who we are in this beautiful world.

DORJEE LHATOO

A long-standing instructor at the Himalayan Mountaineering Institute at Darjeeling in India, he summited Everest as a member of the Indian expedition in 1984.

Unromantic though it sounds, Everest for me began as a jobbing proposition. As I was blessed with good weather and sound health, the climb posed neither difficulty nor surprise and I remained unaware of the impact of summiting until much later.

I have gained profoundly from having climbed Everest, not perhaps in the grand, historical sense of Tenzing and Hillary's ascent, but in a modest and equally profound way. 'Thuji chhe, Chomolungma!' (I am grateful.)

I sometimes wonder whether Everest would have been climbed earlier had it not been for the decree of the Grand Lama of the Rongphu Monastery in the early 1920s. He said, 'Let the sahibs go anywhere they like but you of the inner faith shall not go to the top, for mountain tops are the abode of gods.'

The last two generations of my people strongly believed in that decree and faith, and things changed only with Tenzing.

ANDREW LOCK

The first Australian to climb all 14 8,000-metre/26,246-feet peaks, he summited Everest on 24 May 2000.

Perceived by many as the Holy Grail of mountains, Everest is certainly a challenging and rewarding venture, but for me it was another rung on the ladder, rather than the top step.

It provided an opportunity for reflection on how I'd come to be there and a clearer focus for the future.

The mountain environment embodies both opportunities and obstacles and Everest represents the full spectrum of these. Reaching its summit provided me with a greater awareness of myself and, far from this fulfilling me, Everest has spurred me on to further endeavour.

RODDY MACKENZIE

Australian mountaineer and Himalayan heli-skiing specialist, he summited Everest on 24 May 1989.

I have a theory that people climb for the smell of it. Air at very high altitude smells completely different.

When I reached the South Summit I was suffering from a lack of Spanish olives. I was preoccupied with thoughts of a tin of them sitting in my tent at base camp. This was the result of a very intense dream about olives that was interrupted by the alarm summoning me to our summit attempt. At the South Summit the view of the main summit fascinated me from a mountaineering point of view and all dreaming of olives evaporated.

On the summit I felt a mixture of apprehension and curiosity. It seemed to me that the curvature of the earth was apparent, and I spent some time trying to think of a means to test if this was a real observation or an illusion. My main feeling was of surprise. I am often surprised to find myself in the situations that I end up in.

Many people on the Indian subcontinent believe that the ascent of Everest confers on the climber a greater wisdom in manifold subjects. This is something I do not agree with, but never dispute.

NASUH MAHRUKI

The first Turkish mountaineer to climb an 8,000-metre/ 26,246-feet peak, he summited Everest on 17 May 1995. This 'Seven Summiteer' also helped found Turkey's first search and rescue organisation, AKUT.

After I got the 'Snow Leopard' title from the Russian Mountaineering Federation in 1994, my confidence soared and my ultimate goal became Everest.

The whole expedition – from making contact with a new culture to visiting the roof of the world – was an incredible experience.

I met a goddess on the summit and could only cry before her. I knew that I would never be the same person or the same age again. This bitter reality made me go down on my knees and since then, as Erasmus advised, I make haste slowly.

MAN BAHADUR TAMANG

From the Solu Khumbu district in Nepal, this professional guide and climber has summited Everest three times, in 1992, 1994 and in 1999.

I am very happy on the summit but when the weather changes or the route is very steep, I think maybe I'll be dead, then I worry about my family and children.

One time it was such bad weather that we could hardly see the way and only stayed a couple of minutes. But once we stayed an hour on the summit, took off our hats and gloves, had a drink, took pictures and ate lunch.

Once on the mountain I had a vision of three small Tibetan ladies. When I asked what this means, my Sherpa friends said that it was not a dream. These are the gods of Chomolungma so you must make pujas [prayers].

❄ JUERG MARMET

Number three on the Everest Register (ordered by date of ascent), Swiss mountaineer Juerg Marmet climbed Everest on 23 May 1956.

After a horrible, stormy night at 8,300 metres (27,230 feet), progress was slow in the morning. Suddenly the wind dropped to almost nothing and we enjoyed ascending the ridge, including the Hillary Step, as if we were climbing in the Swiss Alps. It was warm and pleasant. As we had sufficient oxygen on our way up, our perception and judgement were undisturbed and we did not feel fatigued.

The view over Tibet was fabulous as a result of the extremely dry air. In the south-east the monsoon clouds were slowly rising until finally we were caught by the mist and opted to descend in poor visibility after one and a half hours of an unbelievable feeling of detachment, freedom and space.

DANIEL MAZUR

The American mountaineer must have created a record when summiting Everest on 10 October 1991, less than three weeks after meeting and signing up with his new Russian climbing partners in Kathmandu.

While visiting a Kathmandu climbing shop I met a 53-year-old Russian named Roman Giutashvili. I asked where he was going and he said, 'To Everest.' I asked about joining his team and he said it might be possible.

Twenty days later Roman and I stood on the summit in high winds watching the sun set on the surrounding peaks far below, and wondered if we would return alive. We had set off for base camp and arrived after four days of hard hiking behind 30 yaks and 21 porters.

After a sleepless night on the South Col, Roman and I exited a snow-plastered tent and went for the top in high winds and good visibility. Roman was slow, but we stopped often and I made him eat chocolate bars and drink lots of water. By midday the breeze mellowed but it became an icy blast on the arduous Hillary Step. It was so cold on top at 5 p.m. that we did not remove our stiffened oxygen masks while lingering to absorb the incredible panorama of the Himalaya.

Perhaps we stayed too long because on the descent Roman collapsed at 8 p.m. in total darkness. I tried to carry and even drag him, but I was not able to summon enough strength. I dug a snow hole and put him in it with all of our oxygen and a ski pole for a flag.

I promised to return or find help. Roman cried but I knew I could not stay in the hole or I would die.

In a howling ground blizzard, with wind-blown ice grains sandblasting my unmasked cheeks, I stumbled and crawled down a never-ending ice field towards a distant, flickering light. When I came to the tent I collapsed on icy snow and cried out. The door zipped open and I rolled in. Inside were our two very surprised Russian team mates, Alexsei Klimin and Gennady Copieka.

After pouring warm tea down me and trying to understand my nearly incoherent babble, Alexsei went to look for Roman and came back after two hours alone. I wept, knowing my friend was dead. Gennady went next with a very bright headlamp, and in three hours Roman was in the tent, alive and uninjured.

Roman and I made our way down to base camp glad to be alive and stunned at making the summit. Back in Kathmandu I found out that he was the first Soviet Georgian and the second-oldest climber at the time to reach the top. Because of childhood tuberculosis, Roman had only had the use of one lung since the age of 10.

I find it hard to believe that this *accidental* climb occurred, but mostly I am in awe of Roman's courage.

REINHOLD MESSNER

Italian mountaineer and member of the European Parliament, he was, along with Austrian Peter Habeler, the first to climb Everest without oxygen, on 8 May 1978. Messner returned to complete a solo summit of Everest on 20 August 1980.

He was the first to climb all of the world's 14 8,000-metre/26,246-feet peaks and has been described as the greatest mountaineer of the twentieth century.

'I am nothing more than a single, narrow, gasping lung, floating over the mists and summits.'

❄️
ELLEN MILLER

A renowned climber and adventurer, she is the first American woman to climb Everest twice. She summited from the Tibetan side on 23 May 2001, and on 16 May 2002 completed her second ascent, from Nepal.

'Good Morning Everest' was our radio signal to wake and prepare for what I considered to be the culmination of all of my days and years in the mountains.

The sky was starry, but it was freezing cold at Camp 4, at an altitude of 8,320 metres (27,300 feet).

Steps, breaths, feeling bulky in my down suit, headlamps, crampons on rock, old tattered fixed rope, time to change the oxygen cylinder and the old Chinese ladder. Focus, focus, focus, during what were the most intense 12 hours of my life.

Heady thoughts as a beautiful sun rose over the roof of the world. At about 9 a.m., Phurba Sherpa turned and told me with a big smile that there was no place higher to climb on earth.

Everyone who makes the journey up Everest is looking for something, For me, perhaps it was a justification of my unconventional, vagabond lifestyle. Before descending, I squinted, looking out at the Tibetan plateau 4,265 metres (14,000 feet) below, trying to see the elusive curve of the earth. What I glimpsed instead was perhaps the curve of my own soul.

❄ SIMONE MORO

A prominent Italian mountaineer and guide, he has summited Everest four times, in 2000, 2002, 2006 and 2010.

The second time I summited Everest – which I term the third Pole – I was again filled with almost childish enthusiasm. It was like being on the threshold of the full power of the planet, and I was a mere dot on the horizon.

Twenty years ago I shared my first timid climbing experiences with my father, but the flame of wonder in my eyes and joy in my heart lit by mountaineering has not dimmed. This rare vertical experience at the summit of Everest confirmed to me once more that in a few seconds you can live and learn more than in a much larger chunk of time.

---
*

CHRIS MORRIS

American mountain and river guide, who summited Everest on 25 May 2001.

I went to Everest a bit of a sceptic because of the hype and commercialism surrounding it. I returned a spiritual, more humble man. I don't mean to say that I found religion there. But as we waited out storms, witnessed the awesome size and power of the place, and watched as other parties retreated in failure, nagging doubts crept into my mind.

Time and time again we were pushed back down the mountain by the high winds of the jet stream which had parked itself over the summit. It was during a rest day with only three weeks left to climb that I had a sudden feeling of peace and confidence. I told my climbing partners that there was no doubt in my mind that we would be allowed to summit.

The mountain gods were smiling on us. I could feel it as sure as I could feel the sun and wind.

❄
PAT MORROW

This Canadian adventure filmmaker and mountaineer summited as a member of the first Canadian Everest expedition, on 7 October 1982.

Standing atop the world's highest summit was certainly an achievement for me, and for my team. But in the big picture, it was simply part of a continuum of equally fulfilling climbs and adventures that have helped to shape my worldview.

The crass commercialisation of Everest that began with the deregulation of the numbers of teams allowed on the mountain in the 1990s has degraded the experience for those attempting the peak now. Images of Sherpas and Western climbers jostling for positions on ropes that are now fixed all the way from base camp to the summit have taken away any mystique the mountain may have had.

GREG MORTIMER

One of the first two Australians to climb Everest on 3 October 1984, he was also the first Australian to climb both Everest and K2.

The view is tattooed on the underside of my eyelids. I carry it with me everywhere like a secret window.

At the time, I was dizzy with tiredness, I was legless, and overwhelmed by the thought of getting all the way back down to base camp alive. But now, I can close my eyes and see the faint curve of the earth, the inkwell blue sky at the edge of outer space and the arrowhead silhouette of the Big E stretching for 100 kilometres (62 miles) across brown Tibet.

It just so happens that the highest point on earth is right there at the absolute limit of where humans can exist. I have become fascinated by that thought.

What a perilous balancing act we humble humans live.

HUGH MORTON

American house-builder and climber, he summited Everest on 15 May 1992.

I first viewed Everest in 1986 from a small peak while on a trek in the Himalaya. As I sat enthralled by the huge black behemoth rising majestically against the cobalt blue sky, I felt a strange mystical voice in the depths of my mind that challenged me, like the mythical Sirens, to come and try to scale its slopes.

It was an obsessive feeling that would haunt me for the next five and a half years and prod me to master the skills of mountaineering as if I were preparing for the Olympics. It was a long ordeal, but a gratifying honour when finally in 1992 I stood on the top of the world with Todd Burleson, Pete Athans and Keith Kerr, and looked down upon the same brown peak from which I had first viewed Everest over five years earlier.

MOTI LAL GURUNG

When he summited in May 1993, Moti Lal Gurung was the third Gurung to climb Everest. Since then he has worked as a guide and is a member of the Nepal Police mountaineering rescue team.

It was a very good feeling on the top. Usually only Sherpas go climbing but I followed. I have been on many expeditions and have almost reached the top from every route except the east. I have been 10 or 11 times to the South Summit. We turn back because sometimes the weather is not good, sometimes boss not healthy, boss too old, too young, or not good food. Now I'm a little old but I still like to go.

BRIGITTE MUIR

The first Australian to climb the Seven Summits, she was also the first Australian woman to climb Everest, on 27 May 1997.

In 1988 when I started on my project to climb the highest peak on each continent, I was someone who was good at starting things, but not so good at finishing them.

I swore to myself that I would not stop until I had climbed the 'seven *bloody* mountains', as Jon Muir called them. It took me nine years to complete the quest, with the ascent of Everest on my fourth go. And by the way, I never stood on top of Everest: I sat on it. 'No more up' was my first thought from the summit. I then did a recorded message to all Australians asking them to take care of the country and its wilderness.

The climb gave me the confidence to meet new challenges in my life. If you believe in something, you can make it happen.

JON MUIR

He summited Everest on 28 May 1988. As a member of the Australian Bicentenary expedition Jon has also walked to both Poles and made an unsupported solo crossing (from south to north) of the Australian subcontinent. 'I still feel insignificant,' he says.

When I was 14 years old, I saw the documentary *Everest the Hard Way,* about the first ascent of the South West Face. I decided on the spot that I was going to be a mountaineer and climb Everest. At the time, in 1975, only about 50 people had climbed Everest. I knew I had to do it too.

I summited in 1988, reaching the top alone. I spent one hour up there, and I knew then as I know now that I am a very insignificant part of the universe.

Our expedition made the first Sherpa-less ascent from the Nepalese side.

On the walk out we met the Sherpa Sungdare, who at the time had climbed Everest five times. He shook our hands and said, 'You guys are white Sherpas.' That's the highest compliment I've ever received as a mountain climber.

RONALD NAAR

He was one of Holland's most accomplished mountaineers, with many climbing achievements to his credit. He wrote many books about his mountaineering expeditions and summited Everest on 12 May 1992.

For me Everest has never been a special challenge. As a youngster I dreamed of climbing the major north faces of Swiss Alpine peaks, which I managed after I became a mountaineer. When I accomplished this goal it was time to meet the challenge of the Himalaya and I first chose 'the naked mountain', Nanga Parbat in Pakistan. This long, hard and very dangerous climb was a real landmark in the first 26 years of my life.

I reached the summit of Everest during my third expedition, the first time I had been expedition leader. In one way it was very satisfactory. But it was also a huge disappointment. On that day, 12 May 1992, 31 other climbers also reached the top, and all the hard work was done by one Sherpa, Sonam. We simply followed his trail.

Back home my family and climbing companions pressed me to be happy with having climbed Everest, and to see the achievement as the peak of my climbing career. But that was not the case. A few months later I decided that another high mountain would give me that feeling – K2. When I reached the top of that mountain on 17 July 1995 strangely enough I experienced the sensation that I had hoped to find on Everest.

MOHANANDAS NAGAPPAN

A member of the first successful Malaysian Everest expedition, he summited on 23 May 1997.

Two climbers out of the original four Malaysian Everest team had already turned back, leaving only myself and Munisamy Magendran to bear the country's hopes. We were two small, lonely figures in that harsh, white landscape.

The challenge seemed hopeless but eventually the moment we had been waiting for arrived. I heard Magendran's voice over the radio shouting that he had made it to the top. I knew I was just 20 or 30 metres (65 to 95 feet) behind him. I had to carry on.

Finally, I saw Magendran there waiting for me and for the last few steps I gathered all that was left of my strength and went to the top.

NGA TEMBA SHERPA

This famous Nepali climber has summited Everest 10 times and has been on more than 30 Himalayan expeditions.

I find it interesting to climb with foreign friends. Friendship is very important to us Sherpas. I have also taken many Sherpa friends to the mountain, including my son Rinchen. He got within 50 metres (165 feet) of the summit but had to turn back as it was too late.

I am proud he has now done a Master's degree in alternative healing as well as running the family trekking company.

WALDEMAR NICLEVICZ

On 14 May 1995 Brazilian mountaineer Waldemar Niclevicz became the first to fly his country's flag on the summit of Everest.

One needs to discover the Himalaya within, to stop getting lost in the snowy fields and to leave in search of the heights of the Everest of one's own being. This is the true meaning of a climb.

Sagarmatha – may your soul reach the heights.

❋

TENZING NORGAY

The legendary 'Tiger of the Snows' made the first ascent of Everest with Edmund Hillary on 29 May 1953.

'I have climbed my mountain, but I must still live my life.'

> – As told to Tashi Tenzing, Tenzing Norgay's grandson.

'You can't see the entire world from the top of Everest, the view from there only reminds you how much more of the world there is to see and learn from.'

> – As told to Jamling Tenzing Norgay, Tenzing Norgay's son.

❈ CATHY O'DOWD

Now living in Andorra, the first South African to climb Everest summited on 25 May 1996. She became the first woman to summit from both Nepal and Tibet when she reached the top of Everest again on 29 May 1999.

My strongest motivation to summit Everest was to find out how high I could go, how much I was capable of. Only when I finally stood on the South Summit and looked past the Hillary Step was I certain that I could reach the top. The summit brought a wonderful surge of elation, combined with a continued wondering, 'If I have not reached my limits yet, how much further can I go?'

Spread out below me were hundreds of the world's most magnificent mountains, thousands of new challenges and opportunities.

Standing on Everest's summit I realised that I was capable of much more than I gave myself credit for, that the limits on my life were largely self-imposed. An incredible planet lay before me, waiting for me to take action to discover it.

❄
JOBY OGWYN

On 12 May 1999 aged 24, he became the youngest American to climb Everest and has since been credited as one of the youngest people ever to climb all Seven Summits.

At 8,500 metres (28,000 feet) the snow conditions became difficult. I was alone and ahead of the other climbers. At that moment I realised I was the highest person on earth and I could see the summit. Willie Benegas from Argentina soon joined me and we took turns punching through the deep snow. I felt enormous relief when we reached the summit. I felt as if the weight of the world had been lifted from my shoulders.

Then, as I looked around on this clear and beautiful summit day I felt scared. I saw just how high I was and knew I could not linger too long. We stayed on the summit for almost an hour, taking pictures and marvelling at the view. It was difficult to leave this magical place and I got down on my knees and prayed, thanking God for this gift and asking for safe passage back down the mountain.

HARALDUR ÖRN ÓLAFSSON

The Icelandic adventurer accomplished a long-standing dream when he skied to both the North and South Poles and climbed all the Seven Summits in one year. He climbed Everest on 16 May 2002.

To me Everest was like a mystical mountain from a different world. So taking the last few steps to the summit was my biggest moment in climbing, and it was like walking into space.

I felt more like an astronaut than a climber, looking down on the Himalayan giants and the valleys below. It was a joyful moment and I felt a great sense of achievement and relief.

Everest is a gigantic mountain that you must stay focused on all the time. You have to push hard and have luck on your side but the rewards are great. I will never forget it.

MICHAEL OTIS

An American marketing manager who summited Everest on 19 May 2001, on his first Himalayan expedition.

For me, the truest joy is real adventure, and the best gratification in life is the best adventure you can have. I also believe the best rewards come from the most work and sometimes the biggest risks.

Although climbing the North Ridge unguided was the result of my achievement goal, I cannot stress enough that a great support group and Sherpa team made this first summit of the new millennium a very spectacular success.

BACHENDRI PAL

The first Indian woman mountaineer to summit Everest, on 23 May 1984, she also led a distinguished Indo-Nepalese women's team in 1993 that put no fewer than 18 climbers on the summit.

My excellent fitness and resolute determination to uphold 'woman power' motivated my 'do or die' battle to the summit.

In seconds I was on top of the Hillary Step and continued steadily on to the frozen slope, which was hard and brittle as sheets of glass. A few steps later I saw that there was no further upward climb.

My heart stopped. I stood on top of Everest, the first Indian woman to have done so.

Ang Dorjee, my Sherpa sirdar, and I anchored ourselves securely with our ice axes. That done, I sank on my knees and, putting my forehead on the snow, kissed Sagarmatha's crown. Without getting up, I took out the image of Durga Ma [the Hindu Goddess of Power] and my Hanuman *Chalisa* [Hanuman is the Hindu God of Strength] from my rucksack. I wrapped these in a red cloth and, after saying a short prayer, buried them in the snow.

I congratulated Ang Dorjee for his second ascent of Everest without oxygen. He embraced me and whispered, 'You climb good – very happy, Didi.' Didi in Hindi means sister.

PEMBA NURU SHERPA

This trekking and mountaineering guide from the Khumbu region of Nepal summited Everest in 1992 and 1993.

When I first got to the top, I was sure I was not going to survive. I felt only 5 per cent hope of getting back alive and 95 per cent certainty I would die.

PEMBA TENZI SHERPA

As a member of eight Everest expeditions, Pemba Tenzi Sherpa, from the Solu Khumbu region of Nepal, has reached the summit three times: on 25 May 1996, 25 September 1997 and 29 May 1999.

Foreigners pay a lot of money to climb Everest and become very happy when they reach the top. Some get tears in their eyes, some cannot hold their emotion. It is important to do pujas [prayers] before climbing Sagarmatha.

On the summit I give thanks to my guru and think of my family. I still remember the year 1996 when many people died, but I have always been lucky, not having had even a single accident. We treat Everest as a god, but sometimes people do disrespectful things there, which I believe that it does not allow.

PERTEMBA SHERPA

A member of the Sherpa board of the Himalayan Trust and one of Nepal's most distinguished expedition leaders, Pertemba Sherpa has summited three times, in 1975, 1979 and 1985.

As a boy I remember the wonderful stories told by the old Sherpas and thinking: 'How is it possible to climb up into the sky where only the gods and goddesses can live?'

Most Sherpas work with expeditions as a job. It is hard and dangerous. Would you want your son to climb?

Almost half of those killed on Everest have been Sherpas. We have shared our mountains and fresh air with explorers, climbers and tourists. It is important for everyone to help keep the environment clean and respect wildlife and nature.

ANDY POLITZ

The American mountain guide had an unexpected meeting with his friend, another remarkable US climber, on the summit of Everest on 15 May 1991.

On the summit I set out to get some sponsor photos, which at 8,850 metres (29,035 feet) without oxygen gives a unique insight into hypoxia.

At one point, I looked down into Nepal and the South East Ridge only to be surprised by another climber coming up through the clouds. He was startled to see someone looking down at him. He was also climbing without oxygen and was tiring.

The other thought I had, remembering six years of attempting to summit Everest, was: 'He could take my picture.' The hero was nudged out by the ego.

Through scudding cloud I saw that the colour and design of his clothing were unmistakably French. I do not speak French.

As this Frenchman was taking his last steps to the summit, I made the international hand signal for, 'Stop and I'll take your picture.' While I was struggling to focus the camera he looked hard at me and exclaimed, 'Andy!' It was my dear friend Ed Viesturs, on his second ascent of the mountain.

MAURICIO PURTO

This Chilean doctor, filmmaker and climber completed the Seven Summits and was one of the first Chileans to climb Everest when he summited on 15 May 1992.

Everest is a symbol of grandeur and magnificence.

I projected on to Everest my desires, perhaps in a way my wish to become close to that magnificence, to have an 'Everest touch'.

A promise of redemption, an initiation, a quest for our limits, or a journey to the throne of the gods?

For me it was a long and hard pilgrimage from here to there, to the top.

We can describe it in statistical terms or as a savage arena for our egos, looking perhaps for transcendence, for godliness. But I try to concentrate on the experience itself, and the Everest feeling of gratitude that pervaded me just before the summit and that lives on inside me. I was privileged to visit the top of the world, and I regard it as a gift.

❄ GEOFF ROBB

Australian climber Geoff Robb summited Everest on 27 May 1999.

Heading up towards the ridgeline we left most others behind and it was a leap-frogging game with the ten Tibetans, me and Karsang Sherpa. We were fortunate to get to the top of the second step with no one in front just as the dawn was breaking. The sunrise was majestic. The Tibetans steamed past us on the summit pyramid, and it seemed crowded on top as they took their group photos in triumph.

I reached the top at 6.45 a.m. and spent half an hour there, unfurling the Australian flag and taking my photos. The grandeur of the view was only briefly appreciated as my brain had been conditioned to think that getting to the top was only halfway. The three who had died in the previous two weeks had all spent a long time on top.

Getting back to the North Col was a relief, but I didn't have enough strength to get down to that beer at advance base camp until the next morning.

DAVE RODNEY

The author, speaker and filmmaker known to his Nepalese friends as 'Sherpa Dave' is the only Canadian climber to summit Everest twice: on 13 May 1999 and 24 May 2001.

An explosion of infra-red shoots the colours of the spectrum from the horizon to the heavens and a surreal Tibetan sunrise greets me, from far below. As I slowly, carefully turn around, Chomolungma traces her perfectly symmetrical black silhouette upon the Nepalese Himalaya. This is both the furthest from human help and the closest to outer space that I will ever be. That was my experience 'on top of the world', the second time.

The first summit was the fulfilment of the life wish that began as I gazed at my Swiss grandfather's painting of an alpine setting on the wall of his prairie home. Although I was slowed down for a time by a ski-jumping accident – I broke my back in six places and also required four knee operations – nothing could stop me from climbing. But my first summit dream became a nightmare when my team mate, Michael Matthews, lost his life in a blinding blizzard.

That is part of the reason why I had to go back.

The true test in life comes after Everest. We cannot survive on top for long anyway, and surely it is the people and the valley below which sustain us. As our Sherpa friends say, 'When you get to the top, keep climbing!'

JUAN PABLO RUIZ

A former specialist in natural resources for the World Bank, the Colombian mountaineer summited Everest on 24 May 2001.

I reached the summit with Marcelo Arbelaez, my eternal friend, and we hugged each other.

A journalist asked me if reaching the summit was a matter of being a 'superman'. I told him that it was not. Everest is for everyone and is the result of perseverance. The mountain teaches us to evaluate what is essential in life and what is unnecessary, that there are no first and second prizes, and that achievements in a team are social, not individual.

Everest allows me to transmit the lessons learned in the mountains, and is a story and legacy for my grandchildren. It may be the only inheritance that I will take to my grave, the rest I leave to life.

NAZIR SABIR

The renowned mountaineer and adventurer who was the first Pakistani climber to summit Everest, and the second to summit K2, which he climbed from a new route – the West Ridge – in 1981. He summited Everest on 17 May 2000.

My chief motivation in climbing Everest was to pay homage to all those friends of mine who gave their lives in pursuit of their dreams and now rest there in eternal sleep. These include Yasuo Kato, Akira Ube, Toshiaki Kobayashi, Junichi Futagami, Rob Hall and Scott Fischer. I was scheduled to be on what became Scott's and so many others' fatal expedition to Everest in 1996.

I saw these people very clearly in my mind at every step as I was going up the moonlit slope.

But once I stepped on the summit, I felt relieved of a burden and some kind of responsibility. I took off my mask to breathe the very pure air my friends had breathed in their last moments. I felt at one with them and it was with a light heart that I climbed down.

DOUG SCOTT

The first British climbers to summit Everest, and via the South West Face, on 24 September 1975, were Doug Scott and Dougal Haston. Doug is a legendary mountaineer and renowned writer, lecturer and photographer with a string of first ascents, including numerous 8,000-metre (26,246-feet) Himalayan peaks. His main focus now is to raise funds for Community Action Nepal, the Himalayan charity he founded. (Dougal Haston died in an avalanche in Switzerland in 1977.)

It was unusual for me to experience a calm prescience that Dougal and I would make it up to the summit of Everest. There were none of the usual doubts and worries about the weather, snow conditions, my partner's fitness or my own performance on this summit day as there had been on other mountains. There was only the certain feeling that all would be well, that we should keep on pushing up despite Dougal's oxygen system icing up, the difficulties of the yellow rock step, waist-deep powder snow up to the South Summit, a sugar-like snow on the Hillary Step and the passing of day into night as we came up to the main summit.

It was just above the Hillary Step that I experienced a curious out-of-body sensation where part of my mind separated from my tired self and gave me protective advice from above my left shoulder. I was directed away from the cornices hanging over the Kangshung Face and I was advised to slow down and get a good rhythm going rather than stumbling through the crusty snow. I saw myself react positively to this advice from above – which caused me no surprise until I was reflecting on the climb back on the Western Cwm.

We did not make it back to our Camp 6 that night. We did not arrive on the summit until 6 p.m. when there was an amazing sunset with the sun moving down behind strands of cloud. We took a good rest, watching this and looking down at the cloud billowing in the valleys below and across to other peaks all lit up in the setting sun until the sun went down and out as if someone had turned the light off. We went into retreat at 7 p.m. but by the time we had reached the South Summit we were completely out of light and oxygen.

Calling on previous experience, we quite naturally started to dig into a bank of snow and created a cave in which we sat out the long night, rubbing our hands and feet for we had no sleeping bags and the little gas stove was all used up by midnight. It was a long night with shifts of attention from the practical matter of keeping warm into conversations springing from the subconscious. Dougal had a long conversation with Dave Clarke our equipment officer who was actually down in the Western Cwm. The way Dougal was talking, it was as if Dave was right there in the cave with us. They were discussing the relative merits of various sleeping bags. Obviously this manifestation was the result of Dougal not having one.

I was wondering about Dougal. Perhaps he was

about to flip into cerebral oedema? But then I found myself having conversations with my feet as if they were two separate, quite distinct personalities there in the cave. The net result of this was that I put extra effort into rubbing life into these cold appendages. In this way we survived the night, and got ourselves down to the Western Cwm the next day without any frostbite – just as I always knew we would!

SHAMBU TAMANG

The first non-Sherpa Nepali climber to reach the summit of Everest, in May 1973 at the age of 17, he was for decades the youngest person to have climbed Everest. He returned and summited again in 1985.

I did not go to break any records or to become famous. I just went. I prayed on the summit, but actually felt quite lethargic.

I do not feel particularly proud of having gone to the summit, but I was determined to prove that any hard-working and determined Nepali can climb if they want to enough. As a child I used to watch the Sherpas come back through my village with big down jackets and expensive boots. Now several Tamangs and Gurungs – non-Sherpas – have summited.

❋
EDWIN SIEW

This adventurer, educator and resident of Singapore summited Everest on 25 May 1998.

My mom was my source of inspiration when she climbed Mount Kinabalu in Sabah in the mid-1940s, and it is her courage and strength that have spurred me on.

It was right after the legendary Hillary Step that I was challenged with the longest 100 metres (330 feet) I have ever walked in my life. Just as the first few rays of dawn emerged from the Tibetan plateau, I finally set foot on the top of the world. The 45 minutes on the summit was well spent. No one celebrated alone; the team rejoiced as one.

Being a Buddhist, I have always believed in the mountain gods. To me, we can never conquer a mountain in any sense; you have to find the right time when the giant is either asleep or in the right mood to celebrate with you at the top.

ERIC SIMONSON

One of America's most accomplished mountaineers, he summited Everest on 15 May 1991.

I've been to Everest nine times, and each time was very different. Four times I made 8,750 metres (28,700 feet), but only in 1991 did I actually stand on top, via the North Ridge.

I learned just as much from the unsuccessful climbs as I did when I finally made it, on my third try. It was everything I hoped for, and was in no way anti-climactic. The summit day was beautiful on the way up, but it started snowing before we got to the summit. We only spent a couple minutes on top, took a few photos, and started down. It was a whiteout all the way back to high camp. When we reached it the clouds started to break apart, and in the few minutes before it got dark there was a glorious sunset. It was a perfect climb.

❋
BYRON SMITH

When the Canadian climber summited Everest on 21 May 2000, he spoke live on television from the top to his country's Prime Minister.

Looking down from my vantage point towards Namche Bazaar I could see flashes of lightning. The stars were so bright and plentiful, it seemed like you could reach up and grab one in your hand.

As the sun rose I saw the magnificent pyramid shadow of Everest being cast into Nepal. It was a picture of beauty.

I made my way towards the goal I had set years before. I could see some of my Sherpas walking down towards me from the summit. The wind was blowing fiercely. Later Lhakpa Tshering and Ang Dorjee said it was at more than 85 knots, or around 98 miles per hour (158 kilometres per hour).

When I reached the top I called base camp and said, 'I can't go any further . . . I'm on top of the world.' It was great to have the summit all to ourselves.

You can be and do anything you want in life, if you believe in yourself and want it badly enough. Success is an attitude.

SONAM GYALZEN SHERPA

This former president of the Nepal Mountaineering Association was one of the first Nepali climbers to reach the summit of Everest, on 7 May 1973. He is highly respected in his profession as a mountain guide.

I was in the second summit team, the only Nepali climber with three Italians. We headed into a strong storm and had to stop between gusts of wind so were very slow going up. We arrived on the summit at 2.30 p.m. and ran out of oxygen at the South Summit on the way down. When we reached the high camp at 10 p.m., all the tents had blown away except one. As there was no room for me, I stood outside in the snow all night. I got frostbite but did not lose any fingers or toes.

The next day was sunny and the support team came from the South Col to rescue us. I was very tired. It was only after we returned to base camp that I really appreciated how happy I was to have reached the top.

❊
KATJA STAARTJES

The first Dutch woman to summit Everest, on 13 May 1999, was climber and author Katja Staartjes.

In contrast to the rest of the climb, on the last metres before the summit I felt as if I was levitating.

The mountains, and in particular the ascent of Everest, have both given and taught me very much about enjoyment, perseverance, stretching your limits, patience, letting things go, and feeling spiritual.

I love life during expeditions because you are at one with nature, have strong bonds with team members and life is so simple. You concentrate completely on just one thing: the mountain.

DAWSON STELFOX

Architect and mountain guide, he was the first Irishman to summit Everest, on 27 May 1993. As he has both Irish and British nationality he was also the first British climber to summit Everest from the North Ridge since Mallory and Irvine's disappearance in 1924.

We are by nature collectors, measurers, organisers; sorting the chaos of nature into the tallest, deepest, fastest. It was therefore inevitable that Everest should become a symbol rather than a mere mountain.

On the first Irish expedition to Everest, to the North Ridge, we pretended we were just climbing a mountain, without acknowledging or comprehending the immense symbolic importance our success would have in Ireland.

For a brief moment in 1993, my reaching the summit of Everest held out a glimpse of a brighter future for our troubled island. If climbers from all parts of the country, from both religions and none, could work together to elevate me to the highest point in the world, then surely there was no cause in Ireland worth killing for.

The British Queen met the Irish President for the first time ever the day after I reached the summit. Later, a Belfast Lord Mayor made the first ever official visit to Dublin to welcome us home.

It was not long before the realities of sectarian murder broke through this rosy glow, but that cannot take away from the power of Everest.

REBECCA STEPHENS

The first British woman to summit Everest, on 17 May 1993, is an acclaimed writer and journalist.

I felt a brief moment of elation, drowned out in a second by an all-consuming fear. We had to get back down that hill, and quickly! But my memories are sweet: of peering down on the surrounding glaciers and peaks; of feeling so small, yet so big; of my Sherpa companions, Ang Pasang and Kami Tchering, and their joy. It makes me warm still, to think of it.

MARIJA STREMFELJ

One of a Slovenian couple who summited Everest together on 7 October 1990. Andrej Stremfelj had previously summited on 13 May 1979.

My husband and I spent a whole hour on top of Everest without oxygen. I felt very happy and had the intense realisation that you could love everyone in the world, even those who do not love you in return. I had tears in my eyes as I surveyed the magnificent whiteness, the mysterious landscape of Tibet and the tiny strips of shining glaciers.

I wondered what it was all about. Later I knew that I had experienced the real meaning of life up there in the presence of God.

SEAN SWARNER

A member of the Cancer Climber Association, this American climber summited Everest on 16 May 2002.

I reached the summit of Everest and cried like a baby. I am the first cancer survivor to stand on the top of the world, and that thought, that moment of being eye to eye with the stars, would remain a part of me for the rest of my life.

I made this trek for cancer patients and survivors and anyone whose life has been touched by this disease. I carried all these people inside my heart and on a flag to the summit. They were my inspiration, my driving force and my companions. I hope they will learn as I did that any dream is within reach.

JUNKO TABEI

*This Japanese climber was assured of a place in the history
books when she became the first woman to climb Everest.*

At 12.35 p.m. on 16 May 1975, Ang Tshering Sherpa
and I reached the summit. It had been really hard to take
each step forward. However, I knew that the moment to
end the steps would arrive. When I reached the summit, rather than simply feeling the joy of conquering
the mountain, I felt that at last I did not have to take
another single step. The summit was a narrow place, but
it was also a beautiful, natural world of ice and snow
devoid of artificial objects.

GEOFFREY TABIN

The physician and mountaineer, who was a member of the historic American Kangshung Face expedition in 1983, later returned and summited Everest on 2 October 1988. He has devoted considerable time to carrying out and teaching eye surgery in Tibet, Bhutan, Sikkim, Northern Pakistan and throughout Nepal.

Everest screwed up my life, and then made it right again.

I was a first-year medical student at Harvard when the telephone call came: 'Do you want to go to Tibet to climb the last unclimbed face on Everest?'

I joined a team to make the first attempt on the Kangshung Face. We didn't make it, but it put Everest under my skin. It also got me kicked out of medical school. I was eventually taken back. Then the phone rang again.

This time, in 1983, six of my team mates reached the top, but the weather changed before I could try for the summit.

Then, that darn phone rang again. I returned to Everest and was the token male to summit on the team that placed the first two American women on top of Everest.

The actual summit day was pure pleasure. Just after 8 a.m. in a cloudless sky, I was alone on the summit. Half an hour later three Sherpa friends arrived and then Peggy Luce, the second American woman. Stacy Allison had made it to the top two days earlier.

When I returned home, doors opened and my life and perspectives have changed since I heard Everest's call.

TEMBA TSHERI SHERPA

One of the youngest people to reach the summit of Everest did so on 23 May 2001 when he was 16 years old. In 2000 when he was aged only 15 years and 17 days he first climbed with his family, just missing the summit.

I was very happy when I climbed Sagarmatha because I was very young and I am Nepali. I was in a hurry to get down safely, but not worried. On my first attempt in 2000 we failed due to weather, poor equipment and lack of financial support. I had to spend two days above 8,000 metres (26,246 feet) and that is how I lost five fingers. It was very painful, but I have learned to manage. I was lucky to survive. I believe anyone with strong willpower, conviction and determination can do anything, not only gain victory over Everest.

JAMLING TENZING NORGAY

The son of Tenzing Norgay summited Everest on 23 May 1996, 43 years after his father's ascent.

We Sherpas have long respected our mountain environment, because of all that it provides us. The mountains deliver us water, with which we irrigate our fields. The pastures produce grass and fodder for our livestock, and medicinal plants for curing our bodies. And the cliffs and high valleys offer refuge for spiritual practice, for wonder and reflection. Indeed, the mountains are where our livelihoods and our legends were born.

My father retreated in humility during six previous attempts to climb Chomolungma, and he told me that he was able to reach her summit in 1953 – as a visitor on a pilgrimage – only by virtue of respect for the deities who inhabit the mountain and her foothills. Sherpas feel that some of the many deaths on Everest can be attributed to a lack of respect, and to improper motivation when climbing the mountain. My father asked me to continue the tradition of honour and homage to the Himalaya, for only if we carry genuine respect in our hearts will we be protected.

My father showed me the path to the summit of Everest, and I followed in his footsteps. But he also knew that I would have to find my own way, that I would have to climb the mountain myself. Only when I reached the summit did I fully understand this, and I understood him in a way I had not before.

As I stood on the top of the world, gazing across Nepal's fertile valleys and Tibet's windswept plateau, I felt my father there behind me, off to the side where a patch of rocks meets the snow. He told me he was pleased that I had climbed Everest, and that he knew I would be the son to do it. Later, my uncle told me that this wish was exactly what Tenzing had shared with him, in confidence, years before.

What is the meaning of the few brief moments in human history when people have stood atop Everest or other high peaks? Its meaning depends on the motivation of the person standing there. Those who are prepared to truly see and listen will find something different from, and greater than, what they were seeking. They will find that the spirit and blessings of the mountains can be found, ultimately, within all of us.

❈
TASHI TENZING

The Australian-based climber followed in the footsteps of his grandfather, Tenzing Norgay, and first summited Everest on 23 May 1997. On 16 May 2002 to mark the 50th anniversary of the first Swiss expedition attempt on Everest, Tashi summited with Yves Lambert, son of the 1952 Swiss climbing leader Raymond Lambert.

Everest is like a member of my family. We have photographs of her on our walls and my life has been driven by my grandfather Tenzing's and Hillary's historic climb and my own dream to one day stand on top. She is my mountain, my Chomolungma. I feel a part of her and she of me. Everest made me learn my lesson the hard way by taking the life of my Uncle Lobsang in 1993 when we attempted to climb together. It was a painful time but when the time was right she called me back and I knew in 1997 that she would permit me to reach the summit.

For Everest is a mountain of dreams, some fulfilled and many lost. She is a living thing, not stone and ice. I consider myself blessed to see the world from her summit and I can only echo my grandfather's words, 'Thuji cche, Chomolungma' – I am grateful.

RICARDO TORRES-NAVA

*This Seven Summiteer and mountain guide was the first
Mexican climber and the first Latin American to summit
Everest, on 16 May 1989.*

Everest was my staircase to heaven as I summited without pressure from the media or sponsors. I was the underdog with everything to gain and nothing to lose. I was crying with joy and I saw God's hand in all its glory.

Everything changed up there because I found my true self and realised that one has a responsibility to leave something behind for others. That is the secret of immortality: to live through one's deeds and memories. Now I live more fully and I cherish every moment, every person, and every summit.

MIKE TRUEMAN

After being deputy leader and leader on two previous Everest expeditions, the former British Gurkha army officer summited Everest on 13 May 1999.

Only a masochist would enjoy the agony of climbing Everest. Ascending from the South Col through the night is a monotonous, torturous experience.

Technically the Hillary Step must have been an aesthetically pleasing challenge in 1953; now it is more often a strength-sapping tug using a number of the old fixed ropes. Above the step the angle lessens and at last the summit is there to be gained.

It was at this point that I felt my only soaring moment of elation.

At the summit I quickly took photographs and all I could think about was returning safely. The climb would only end when I reached home.

I passed a young British climber at the Hillary Step as I descended and he continued upwards. Hours later he would perish in a storm.

When I think of that day my first feeling is of sadness and I often consider whether Everest is worth it or not.

❄
DENIS URUBKO

On 24 May 2000 Kazakhstan's Denis Urubko summited Everest. His remarkable high altitude climbing achievements in the Pamirs would rival the efforts of most Olympic athletes.

My aim was to summit without oxygen or Sherpa support. In the spring of 2000 we arrived at the foot of Everest. After setting up the camps we were caught by a storm on the South Col where we spent three nights at 8,000 metres (26,246 feet). And although we were already exhausted we made an attempt. The weather was terrible and on the top my emotions were slightly deadened, but I still remember the rejoicing that filled my soul. The goal was reached in an honest way with sporting principles that I have remained faithful to. Being at the summit was a moment of truth and with Everest in my heart I became a stronger person.

RUDY VAN SNICK

After reaching the South Col four times in 1989, he returned to Everest the following year and became the first Belgian to summit, on 10 May 1990.

In 1989 during the first Belgian Everest winter expedition, 150 metres (490 feet) below the summit, I was faced with the appalling decision of whether to attempt to summit or assist my Sherpa companion Dorje Lhakpa. There was no choice. I tried hard, but tragically Lhakpa died before we could get him to safety. Three months later I was again ascending the upper flanks of Everest. 'Mister South Col' was my nickname. I returned to the South Col no less than four times but was unable to summit.

In May 1990 my fortunes changed. It was agreed among the team that each climber would be self-sufficient so on the summit day I climbed without any feeling of dependence on my climbing companions.

By climbing Everest I recognised the wealth of opportunities that it created. It has meant a life pursuing my ambitions as a mountain guide and has opened the door to many other possibilities.

STEPHEN VENABLES

One of Britain's most accomplished and respected mountaineers, on 12 May 1988 he became the first British climber to summit Everest without supplementary oxygen after climbing a new route up the Kangshung Face.

Nearly all the publicity surrounding recent Everest expeditions seems to have concentrated on death, disaster and controversy.

My own memories of Everest are very different. I joined a wonderful team. John Hunt was 'honorary leader' of our 35th Anniversary ascent, and Tenzing Norgay's eldest son, Norbu, was on the support team. Our sirdar, Pasang Norbu, sustained us for three months with kindness, laughter and brilliant cooking. His assistant, Kasang Tsering from Kharta, worked wonders. Our doctor, Mimi Zieman, and our photographer, Joseph Blackburn, watched and waited for weeks at base camp. And then there were the climbers: Robert Anderson the unfailing optimist, Paul Teare, the wise man who made us all laugh, Ed Webster, the climbing superstar and romantic dreamer.

As for the mountain, we were on the East [Kangshung] Face, so every dawn was a glorious treat. After the cold, anxious, dark start, it was thrilling to watch the sun explode over the Arun valley, and see our own wall blaze orange, pink, purple and gold, full of promise for another magical day on the mountain.

Climbing Everest was a great adventure. Above all it was fun, and I would not have missed it for anything.

JAIME VIÑALS

After years of training in the Andes mountain range and the European Alps, the first climber from Guatemala summited Everest on 23 May 2001.

In Guatemala we don't have any glaciers or snow and mountains. The main focus is on football and soccer, so there is no space for mountaineering.

My dream was to show that it doesn't matter where you are from, you just need the will to reach your own goals. The team was great and very experienced, and when we reached the summit of Everest, it was the most important day of my life.

We were on the top of the world with very good weather and spent around 30 minutes admiring Lhotse, Makalu, the summit ridge from the south and north, and the Tibetan plateau.

Everest was incredibly important to me, because not only did I reach this great summit: I reached myself.

EVGENY VINOGRADSKY

Russian doctor and mountaineer Evgeny Vinogradsky has summited Everest four times, in 1992, 1995, 1997 and 1998.

For me the summit is not the goal, although it is always a feeling of relief to arrive there safely. But I didn't yell with happiness.

I like the process of climbing, and even though I have been to the top four times I always find something new. It is an experience I dream about repeating.

BERNARD VOYER

This Canadian mountaineer who has reached both the North and South Poles has also completed the Seven Summits. He summited Everest on 5 May 1999.

Very early on I knew the winter wind, the pleasures of sledding, and since then I have been roaming the world in search of the coldest summits.

I have stood at the North and South Poles and completed a world tour via the highest summit on each continent. Everest was my third Pole. There, on the roof of the world, I gathered a bit of snow from the summit in a jar.

Ever since that day I have been constantly looking up at the clouds and thinking of the peaks that rise through them, of the new challenges awaiting me and the beauty of life.

There will always be men who reach summits, step by step. Up there, with icy feet and frosty faces, breathless and exalted in their success, they will look out at the horizon and touch the real sky. But above all, they will be free.

FRITS VRIJLANDT

The celebrated Dutch mountaineer who summited Everest on 17 May 2000 is the only Dutchman to have done so via the North Side.

I approached Everest with respect and I was well aware of being just a small human being. An excellent preparation is very important, but far from a guarantee that you will reach the summit. You have to be mentally ready to go for it, sufficiently experienced, and a brave and careful climber.

Before our summit bid our team agreed that returning alive and without injuries was our main objective. Some people can be blindly obsessed by Everest.

I reached the top after eight hours of climbing. After I contacted base camp and they had congratulated me I replied, 'Thank you, but first I have to come back alive.'

After my return to Kathmandu I felt like a superbeing because I had stood on the top of the world. I still had this feeling when I came back home but soon it faded away. The world or your life doesn't change because you climbed a mountain, even if it is the tallest. But climbing Everest was a spiritual experience for me. It puts your feet back on the surface of Mother Earth.

CHRIS WARNER

One of America's leading mountain guides and educators, who summited Everest on 23 May 2001.

When we reached the summit 20 people were already there. I had been hoping for a bit of solitude, and an opportunity to savour the moment. I couldn't find that on the very top so I descended about 6 metres (20 feet) and sat alone.

I had a collection of mementoes in my pack. I took these out, tied a Buddhist prayer flag to the Catholic Church's crucifix and placed these on the snow. I then pulled out a picture of a paralysed friend who had recently passed away. I let him soak in the views and then asked him, God and the Buddhist gods to protect us on the descent.

As a guide, the weight of my responsibility kept my imagination well grounded. Within three or four minutes, I was on my feet and shepherding my team back towards the safety of advanced base camp.

ERIK WEIHENMAYER

On 25 May 2001 an American mountaineer became the first blind climber to summit Everest. He has since completed ascents of all 'Seven Summits'.

I don't climb mountains to prove to anyone that blind people can do this or that. I climb for the same reason an artist paints a picture: because it brings me great joy.

But I'd be lying if I didn't admit my secret satisfaction in facing those cynics and blowing away their doubts, destroying their negative stereotypes, taking their narrow parameters of what's possible and what's not, and then shattering them into a million pieces.

When those parameters are rebuilt, thousands and thousands of people will live with fewer barriers placed before them, and if my climbs can play a small role in opening doors of opportunity and hope for those who will come after us, then I am very proud of what we were able to achieve.

TOM WHITTAKER

Professional speaker, corporate trainer and president of the non-profit foundation the Wind Horse Legacy, this Welshman and US citizen became the first disabled climber to summit Everest on 27 May 1998.

Black turns to cobalt blue, reflecting gunmetal grey on the snow in front of me. Regretfully, I douse my headlamp.

The Tinkerbell dancing in front of me means more than just a source of light. Perhaps it is the link between my world and the gruelling reality of climbing Everest.

My carbon fibre Flex-Foot prosthesis which gives me bounce when the going is firm is now a ball and chain, and a misstep here would cause a domino effect on my climbing partners Jeff Rhoads, and Sherpas Norbu and Lakpa below.

'Okay, Whittaker, it's time to get it done,' Jeff says.

Just as I abandon all aspirations of ever standing on the roof of the world a wispy string of prayer flags flutters a welcome.

I step with care so as not to catch the crampon on my prosthetic foot in this summit shrine and rocket head first into Tibet. Pulling off the oxygen mask I mutter, 'Who'd have thought it?'

On the summit I sprinkled the ashes of my mentor and friend, Bill March. As I tucked away the purple velvet pouch the physical sensation was akin to sitting inside a car when someone slams the door.

I can't speak with any certainty about God but standing up there on Everest's summit there was no doubt I'd just experienced an energy force leaving my body.

I climbed this mountain for myself and also for everyone who believed in this dream.

KRZYSZTOF WIELICKI

A member of the Polish expedition, he made the first successful winter ascent on Everest on 17 February 1980.

After eight hours of climbing from the South Col I saw Leszek Cichy's raised hands on a long crest. When we reached the summit he shouted into the walkie-talkie, 'We are' – a deep breath – 'we are at the top' – an even deeper breath – 'we are at the top of Everest.'

It was my first 8,000-metre (26,246-feet) peak and there we were, in the middle of nowhere, but we did not feel lonesome.

I was living out not only my dreams but also the dreams of many supporters. One must sometimes climb that high and go that far to comprehend what happiness is.

We left the cross and the rosary from the Pope. We struggled for 20 minutes to remain at the top, then I started thinking about how we had to descend to the South Col that evening and try to find our small camp tent. Nobody was waiting for us there. I could not feel my feet because of frostbite, and the torches were not working any more. The night was falling, people were far away and the wind was picking up. Faith in survival wins.

RICHARD WILCOX

This American mountain guide summited Everest on 15 May 1991.

I was 43 years old when I climbed Everest and proud of the style with which we summited the peak. On summit day I climbed along with Mark Richey, Barry Rugo and Yves LaForest using no harnesses, jumars or fixed ropes. It was the thrill of a lifetime to be alone on the South Ridge and to share the summit of Everest with just my close climbing buddies.

❋
WONGCHU SHERPA

On 14 May 1995 Wongchu Sherpa, from the Khumbu region of Nepal, climbed Everest.

When I stood on the top of Everest I felt that I was inside an aeroplane and looking down on the scenery. It was such a wonderful view from there. I was also feeling a bit warm because of the strong sunshine. I then started to think about returning home safely.

SHARON WOOD

The climbing and ski guide who was the first Canadian woman to summit Everest, on 20 May 1986.

At 8,230 metres (27,000 feet) up in the Hornbein Couloir at the base of the Yellow Band my climbing partner handed me the end of the rope and said, 'Your lead.' Focus replaced trepidation as I poured my all into making the next move – perfectly.

High above, the gale-force winds scoured the flanks of the North Face, funnelling debris down the narrowing couloir as we scraped our way up. The spindrift avalanches parted around our boot tops, and the sound of the snow's passage hissed the words of a dead friend, John Lauchlan, 'Go big or go home.'

Then it was the raspy voice of our leader Jim Elzinga wafting up from the radio tucked deep in my jacket: 'You gotta want it more than it wants you!'

It's evening and the wind is dying: an irresistible invitation to go on.

The sun is setting and we are on top slumped in exhaustion, panting, looking at one another and saying, 'Let's tag the top and get the hell out of here.'

You never conquer the mountain, you conquer a part of yourself.

GLOSSARY

Acclimatisation – ability to adjust to the lack of oxygen at high altitude. Associated with hypoxia (lack of oxygen to brain or lungs).

Advance base camp – the camp above base camp.

The Balcony – a ledge or shoulder located at approximately 400 metres (1,300 feet) above the South Col.

Base camp – literally the camp at the base of the mountain, where the walk-in finishes and the climb begins.

The 'Big Five' – Everest, K2, Kangchenjunga, Lhotse, Makalu (all over 8,000 metres [26,246 feet]).

Bivouac – an overnight shelter in the open.

Camp 1, 2, 3, etc. – Camps fixed by climbing teams on their way to the summit.

Chomolungma – Tibetan for Everest, 'Mother Goddess of the world'.

Chorten/stupa – shrine in memory of a Buddhist saint, a conical stone monument often containing relics or symbolising the natural elements.

Couloir – a steep gully on a mountainside.

Crampon – set of metallic spikes attached to the underside of boots to assist ascent on compact snow/ice.

Eight-thousand-metre (26,246-feet) peaks – the 14 peaks are:

Everest	8,850m (29,035ft)
K2	8,611m (28,251ft)
Kangchenjunga	8,598m (28,208ft)
Lhotse	8,501m (27,890ft)
Makalu	8,463m (27,765ft)
Dhaulagiri	8,167m (26,794ft)
Manaslu	8,156m (26,758ft)
Cho Oyu	8,153m (26,748ft)
Nanga Parbat	8,125m (26,656ft)
Annapurna	8,091m (26,545ft)
Gasherbrum (Hidden Peak)	8,068m (26,469ft)
Broad Peak	8,047m (26,401ft)
Gasherbrum II	8,035m (26,361ft)
Shishapangma	8,013m (26,289ft)

To date all 14 8,000-metre (26,246-feet) peaks have been climbed by 10 mountaineers.

Gurungs/Tamangs – Nepalese climbers, non-ethnic Sherpas.

Hillary Step – an impressive rock/ice gully directly below the summit and technically the hardest section of the summit day ascent along the South East Ridge.

Himalaya – mountain range dividing Nepal and Tibet.

Hornbein Couloir – the upper section of the American route in 1963 that followed the western shoulder and the West Ridge before branching off into Tibet to reach the summit.

Ice axe – axe to assist when climbing on snow and ice.

Jumar – a metal clamp for climbing fixed ropes.

Kangshung Face – the Hidden or East Face of Everest.

Kathmandu – the capital of Nepal.

Khumbu Icefall – the huge mass of ice towers and crevasses that defines the initial stage of the climbing route above base camp.

Lhotse – mountain adjacent to Everest.

Namche Bazaar – major Sherpa village.

1996 tragedy – when nine climbers (including well known guides) were killed during a storm on the summit day of 10 May 1996 – the most climbers to die in a single day on Everest.

North Col – 7,000-metre (22,965-feet) location of camp on the Tibet side, North East Ridge approach to the summit.

North East Ridge – the ridge that defines the final approach to the summit from Tibet.

North Ridge – extension to North East Ridge.

Pujas – prayers often made at the commencement of a climb.

Rongphu Glacier – glacier that marks the approach to Everest from the Tibetan side.

Rongphu Monastery – Buddhist monastery in Tibet, a stage before the base camp (on the Tibetan side).

Sagarmatha – the Nepalese name for Everest, which is a Sanskrit word meaning 'brow of the sky'.

Seracs – A pinnacle or ridge of ice on the surface of a glacier where crevasses intersect.

Seven Summits – the highest peaks in each continent.

Asia	Everest	8,850m (29,035ft)
South America	Aconcagua (Argentina)	6,960m (22,834ft)
North America	McKinley (Denali)	6,194m (20,321ft)
Africa	Kilimanjaro (Uhuru)	5,895m (19,340ft)
Europe	Elbrus (Russia/Georgia)	5,642m (18,510ft)
Antarctica	Vinson	4,897m (16,066ft)
Australasia	Carstensz (Irian Jaya)	4,884m (16,023ft)

Many climbers have opted for the more accessible 2,228 metre (7,310-feet) summit of Kosciusko in the Australian Alps.

To date over 100 climbers have completed the Seven Summits.

Sherpa – ethnic Tibetan now resident in Nepal in the vicinity of Everest.

Sirdar – Nepalese term for the head porter or head Sherpa.

South Col – at 8,000 metres (26,246 feet), the location of high camp on the Nepal–South East Ridge approach to the summit.

South Summit – the lower or false summit of Everest on the South East Ridge approach.

Summit – the height of Everest was until recently 8,848 metres (29,028 feet). This has now been adjusted to 8,850 metres (29,035 feet).

Thyangboche Monastery – famous Sherpa monastery in Nepal several stages from Everest.

Western Cwm – the section of the climb above the Icefall.

The Yellow Band – Everest is composed of three distinctive layers of rock. The third layer begins at 8,380 metres (27,493 feet) and the first 150 metres (492 feet) of that consists of yellow limestone, which is known as the Yellow Band.